PREHISTORIC CREATURES

S0-ARL-421

SUPER
LITTLE GIANT BOOK™ OF

PREHISTORIC CREATURES

DAVID LAMBERT
AND THE DIAGRAM GROUP

Sterling Publishing Co., Inc.
New York

Library of Congress Cataloging-in-Publication Data Available

10 9 8 7 6 5 4 3 2 1

Published in 2006 by Sterling Publishing Co., Inc.
387 Park Avenue South, New York, N.Y. 10016

Created by Diagram Visual Information Limited
195 Kentish Town Road, London, NW5 2JU, England

© 2005 Diagram Visual Information Limited

Distributed in Canada by Sterling Publishing
c/o Canadian Manda Group, 165 Dufferin Street,
Toronto, Ontario, Canada M6K 3H6

Written by	David Lambert and the Diagram Group
Edited by	Denis Kennedy, Gordon Lee
Illustrated by	Graham Rosewarne and
	Pavel Kostal, Kathy McDougall, Coral Mula
Production	Richard Hummerstone
Design	Anthony Atherton, bounford.com,
	Lee Lawrence, Ruth Shane
Picture research	Neil McKenna

Printed in China
All rights reserved

Sterling ISBN 13: 978-1-4027-2593-7
        ISBN 10: 1-4027-2593-0

For information about custom editions, special sales, premium and
corporate purchases, please contact Sterling Special Sales
Department at 800-805-5489 or specialsales@sterlingpub.com.

Foreword

The origins of life on Earth, as much as the origins of the planet itself, still remain a mystery. But the closer we move to the present day the clearer the overall picture becomes. The *Super Little Giant Book*™ *of Prehistoric Creatures* brings to life one aspect of the picture more vividly than ever before.

Scientists can tell when and what kind of creatures lived a long time ago from clues in rocks that hold the creatures' fossils. And this book indeed starts by introducing the reader to fossil proofs of prehistoric life. It then tells you about life in the sea, the land and the air, becoming more specific as the life forms become ever more diverse. The book tells you when the creatures of the ancient past lived, whether they were tiny insects or two-legged predators big enough to swallow humans whole (had they been around at that time!) It tells you whether they were herbivores, as heavy as a herd of elephants, or carnivores, creatures feeding on flesh, with or without bony shields, plates, spikes, or horns. The answers to how they behaved toward one another and how long they lived are also contained within this book.

So the invertebrates, fishes, amphibians, and early tetrapods, reptiles, birds, mammals, and other synapsids have each been given a section of the book with an abundance of data that makes life on Earth at that time seem stranger than fiction. Yet it has all been based on scientific research done over a number of years.

Contents

1. Beginnings and Development

PREHISTORIC TIME

Paleontologists can tell when prehistoric creatures lived from clues in rocks that hold the creatures' fossils. The lowest strata in a stack of layered rocks are usually the oldest, so stratigraphy helps us to work out the relative ages of fossils from different layers. Some rocks contain radioactive elements that gradually change into new elements at a known rate. Measuring the amounts of these elements in the rocks can tell us the actual ages of the rocks and so the actual ages of the associated fossils. This is radiometric dating.

The Earth is more than 4,500 million years old but all prehistoric creatures lived in the last two of Earth's four great time spans called aeons (the last 2,500 million years). Each of the aeons is divided into eras divided into periods. The first known invertebrates emerged in the last period of the Proterozoic Aeon of 2,500–545 million years ago (mya). All other creatures are linked to the Phanerozoic Aeon: 545 mya to the present. Fishes, amphibians, and reptiles appeared during the Paleozoic Era: 545–248 mya. Dinosaurs, birds, and mammals emerged in the Mesozoic Era: 248–65 mya. Mammals and birds have dominated life on land all through the Cenozoic Era: 65–0 mya.

Eon millions of years ago	Era	Period	Epoch
Phanerozoic 545–present	**Cenozoic** 65–present	**Quaternary** 1.8–present	**Holocene** 0.01–present
			Pleistocene 1.8–0.01
		Tertiary 65–1.8	**Pliocene** 5.3–1.8
			Miocene 23.8–5.3
			Oligocene 34–23.8
			Eocene 55–34
			Paleocene 65–55
	Mesozoic 248–65	**Cretaceous** 144–65	
		Jurassic 206–144	
		Triassic 248–206	
	Paleozoic 545–248	**Permian** 290–248	
		*Carboniferous 354–290	
		Devonian 408–354	
		Silurian 438–408	
		Ordovician 505–438	
		Cambrian 545–505	
Proterozoic 2,500–545			

* Mississippian and Pennsylvanian periods in N. America

Fossil proofs of prehistoric life

The kind of animals featured in this book died out long before humans appeared. We know about these prehistoric creatures mainly from the hard parts of their bodies that have survived as fossils in rocks.

Many fossils form like this: A fish (**1**) dies and sinks to the bed of a lake. (**2**) Its flesh decays and disappears. (**3**) Before its bones, too, rot away, mud covers them, shutting out the oxygen needed by bacteria that cause decay. (**4**) Mud layers piling up above the bones turn to rock. Meanwhile, dissolved minerals fill tiny pores in the bones, chemically changing them to hardened fossils reinforced against the weight of rock above. (**5**) Millions of years later, the Earth's crust heaves, lifting the layered rocks as mountains. (**6**) Later still, streams wear down the rocks, laying bare the fossil bones inside.

The best-known kinds of fossil include the remains of shells, bones, teeth, and eggs.

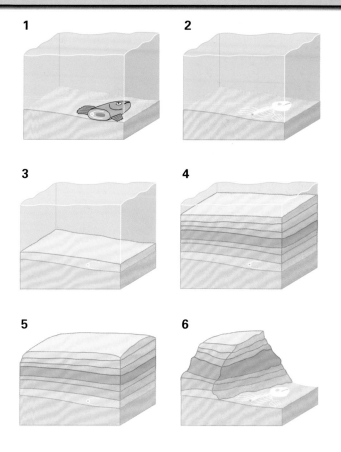

The start of life on Earth

As you can see from this diagram, dinosaurs ruled the Earth for more than 140 million years, but then they became extinct. No one is sure why they disappeared. Some scientists blame a giant rock, an asteroid that came from outer space

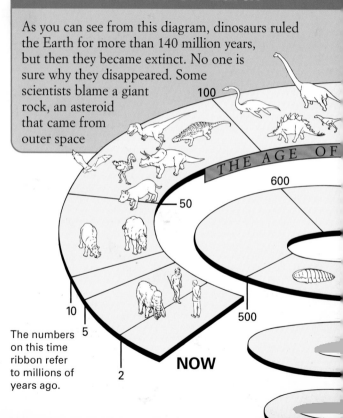

100

THE AGE OF

600

50

10

5

NOW

500

2

The numbers on this time ribbon refer to millions of years ago.

and collided with the Earth. The huge cloud of dust caused by the collision of the asteroid with the Earth may have blocked out light from the Sun, and so many plants and animals would have died as a result.

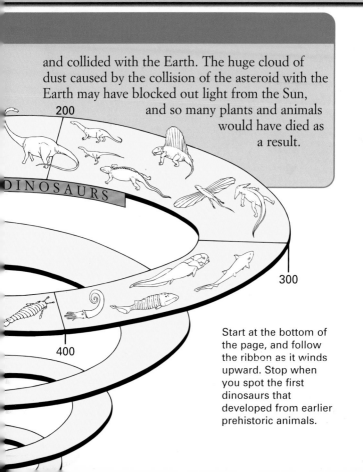

200

DINOSAURS

300

400

Start at the bottom of the page, and follow the ribbon as it winds upward. Stop when you spot the first dinosaurs that developed from earlier prehistoric animals.

Changing lands, and the Triassic Period

For much of the Mesozoic Era, all of the great landmasses lay touching one another; most were warm all year. At first, dinosaurs and other warmth-loving creatures spread everywhere. Later, continents drifted apart and climates changed. Cut off from one another, animal groups evolved differently in different places.

The first part of the Mesozoic Era, the Triassic Period, derives its name from three rock layers formed in Germany at this time, 250–208 million years ago.

The Jurassic Period derives its name from rocks formed in the French and Swiss Jura Mountains at this time, 208–144 million years ago.

The Cretaceous Period derives its name from the chalky layers which formed the floors of some seabeds at this time, 144–65 million years ago.

In the late Triassic world continents lay jammed together. The Tethys Sea **a** separated eastern Laurasia **b** from eastern Gondwana **c**. Dinosaurs could, and did, walk from one part to the other, but they found deserts in the huge inland areas far from the ocean's rain-bearing winds.

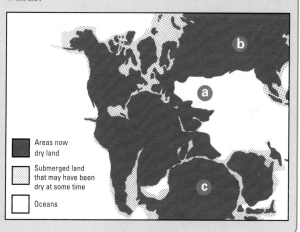

Areas now
dry land

Submerged land
that may have been
dry at some time

Oceans

Changing lands, and the Jurassic and Cretaceous Periods

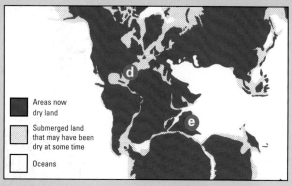

Areas now
dry land

Submerged land
that may have been
dry at some time

Oceans

In the Mid-Jurassic world sea-filled cracks were
opening or widening between some landmasses.
The beginning of the Atlantic Ocean **d** had
started to separate Africa from North America.
India **e** was splitting away from Africa and
Antarctica. Australia had begun to break away
from Antarctica. New types of dinosaur walked
overland to all parts of the world during this
period, and flourished best in plant-rich lands
with rainy seasons.

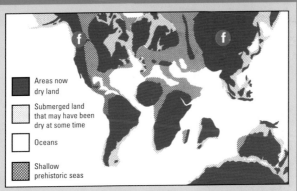

Areas now
dry land

Submerged land
that may have been
dry at some time

Oceans

Shallow
prehistoric seas

In the Late Cretaceous world the continents were
taking on their modern outlines and positions.
Lands once joined had drifted far apart. Also,
shallow seas invaded many regions. These changes
cut off some groups of dinosaurs from others.
New types evolving in what became the landmass
Asiamerica ⓕ could not reach other continents,
and vice versa.

The Precambrian Period

Precambrian time occupied Earth's first 400 million years. Rocks laid down then still largely form the cores of continents. One-celled life forms appeared in seas at least 3,500 years ago. By 32,000 million years ago, blue-green algae had begun enriching the atmosphere with oxygen. In time they made life possible for more complex living things. Soft-bodied, many-celled water animals were burrowing through underwater mud 1,000 million years ago. By 680 million years ago, soft corals, jellyfish, and worms all flourished off sandy shore of South Australia.

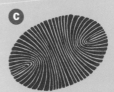

2,500–543 million years ago

a Monera
b Plants
c Invertebrates

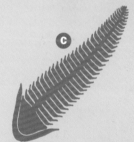

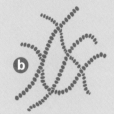

The Cambrian Period

The Cambrian Period gets its name because scientists first studied fossils from the period in Wales, Cambria in Latin. This is the start of the Paleozoic Era, the "age of ancient life." There is one large land mass—Gondwana—along with the smaller, separate continents of Europe, North America, and Siberia.

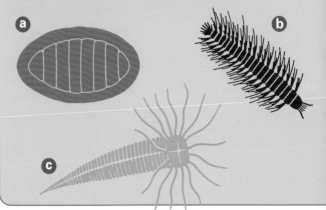

543–490 million years ago

At this time, all life lives in the sea, including backboneless jellyfishes, sponges, starfishes, and worms, all relatives of animals alive today. Some creatures gain the knack of building hard protective shells from chemicals dissolved in the water.

Invertebrates
a Molluscs
b Annelid worms
c Coelenterates
c Annelid worms
d Arthropods

The Ordovician Period

The Ordovician Period is named after the Ordovices, an ancient Celtic tribe of western Wales, where scientists first studied Ordovician fossils. Gondwana and the other continents are closing the ocean gap between them, while ice covers parts of Africa and South America. Shallow seas repeatedly flood North America.

490–443 million years ago

Animals and plants still live only in the sea, many of them resembling their Cambrian ancestors. Trilobites are the most numerous, molluscs develop as bivalves and one-shelled gastropods, while jawless fishes make their first appearance.

Invertebrates
a Coelenterate
b Molluscs
c Enchinoderms
d Tentaculate
e Branchiotreme
f Arthropod

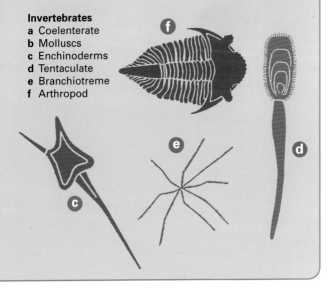

The Silurian Period

The Silurian Period is named after the Silures, an ancient tribe living on the Welsh–English border. During this period, colliding continents raise up mountain ranges in North America and Europe and forge two new supercontinents: Laurasia in the north and Gondwana in the south. Plants and small creatures such as millipedes make their first appearance on land.

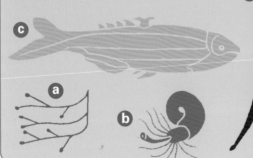

443–417 million years ago

The first jawed fish occur at this time, invading lakes and rivers, although many of them are hunted by giant sea scorpions. Solitary corals build great reefs, and the shallow sea floors support a rich array of sea lilies, lampshells, trilobites, and molluscs.

a Plants
b Invertebrates
c Fish

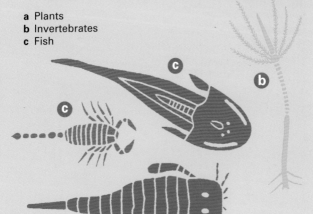

The Devonian Period

The Devonian Period is named from the shales, slates, and sandstone laid down in Devon, England. During this period, Laurasia and Gondwana draw closer together. Sea levels are high and flood Laurasia, while mountains rise where North America and Europe collide. Deep oceans cover the rest of the planet. Climates are warm and mild everywhere.

The Devonian is the age of the fishes. Jawless fish share the waters with the more progressive jawed fishes about to replace them, including huge

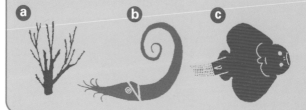

417–354 million years ago

placoderms, primitive sharks, and early bony fishes, the fleshy-finned ancestors of amphibians. On land, the world's first forests appear, as do amphibians and wingless insects.

a Plants
b Invertebrates
c Fish
d Amphibians

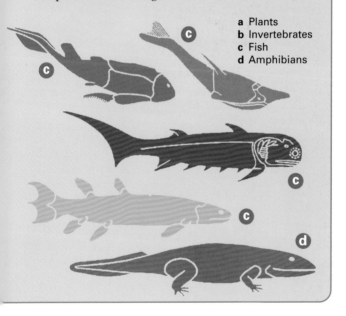

The Carboniferous Period

The Carboniferous Period—the "age of coal"—is named after the thick bands of carbon in the form of coal laid down when shallow seas drowned tropical forests on the two vast continents. Oxygen levels are high, allowing giant, land-based arthropods to evolve. The first reptiles appear, able to lay eggs out of water.

Large amphibians, some as big as crocodiles, lurk on the mudbanks below the tall tree ferns and horsetails. Others hunt fishes in the pools. Those with study limbs walk easily on land, while those with tiny or no limbs swim like eels. Overhead fly giant dragonflies and other insects.

2,500–543 million years ago

a Plants
b Invertebrates
c Fishes
d "Amphibians"
e Reptiles

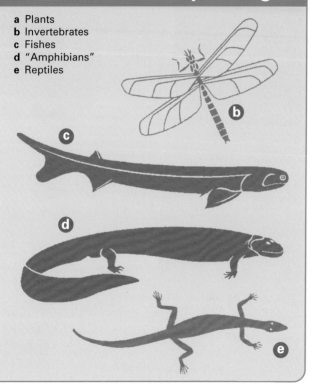

The Permian Period

Fossil-rich rocks near Perm in Russia give their name to the Permian Period. The two vast continents finally merge to form one supercontinent, Pangaea ("all Earth"). At the end of the period, a mass extinction occurs, with perhaps as few as five percent of species surviving, ending the Paleozoic Era.

Reptiles take over from amphibians to dominate life on Earth. Major new insect groups—beetles, bugs, and cicadas—emerge, while the forests are now full of conifers. Bony fish swim in the lakes and rivers, and some find their way into the sea.

290–248 million years ago

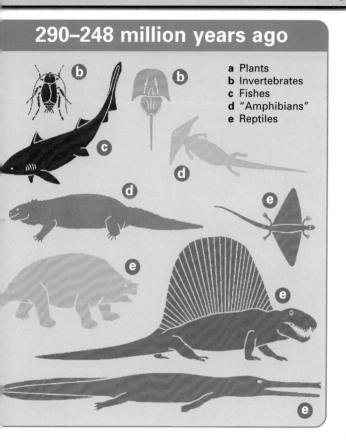

a Plants
b Invertebrates
c Fishes
d "Amphibians"
e Reptiles

The Triassic Period

The Triassic Period—named from the Latin trias (three) after three rock layers from this period found in Germany— marks the start of the Mesozoic Era, the "age of middle life." It is also the age of the dinosaurs. During the Triassic, a narrow seaway begins to separate North America from Europe. The climate is generally warm and dry.

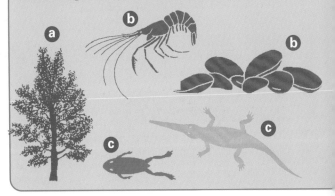

248–206 million years ago

Early saurischian and ornithischian dinosaurs share the land with tortoises, lizards, and the shrewlike eotherian, the first mammal. Above their heads flap winged pterosaurs. Crocodiles swim in the lakes and rivers. Together, the dinosaurs, pterosaurs, and crocodiles—all archosaur reptiles—dominate life for the entire Mesozoic Era.

a Plants
b Invertebrates
c "Amphibians"
d Reptiles
e Mammalian form

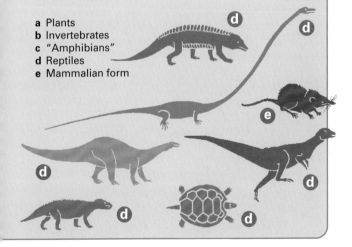

The Jurassic Period

The Jurassic Period is named from rocks formed at this time in the Jura Mountains of France and Switzerland. The Pangaea supercontinent splits up as the Atlantic Ocean forms, while Antarctica, India, and Australia slowly move away. The climate is warm, with no polar ice caps. Sea levels are high worldwide.

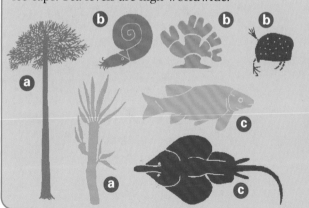

193–136 million years ago

Palmlike bennettitaleans, ferns, and tree ferns flourish during this period. A zoo of dinosaurs evolves to browse on this plentiful vegetation, including armored ornithischian dinosaurs and the mighty saurischian sauropods. The first birds take to the air, joining the pterosaurs.

a Plants
b Invertebrates
c Fishes
d "Amphibians"
e Reptiles
f Birds

The Cretaceous Period

The Cretaceous Period owes its name to the chalk laid down in the shallow seas; creta is Latin for chalk. By now Pangaea has broken up into Laurasia in the north and Gondwana in the south and the continents are taking on their modern outlines and positions. At the end of this period, the dinosaurs and other groups become extinct, ending the Mesozoic Era.

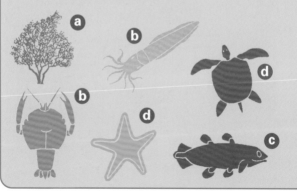

136–65 million years ago

Many modern types of plant and animal appear as the age of the dinosaurs ends. Flowering plants multiply and spread, their well-protected seeds surviving the cool winters. Typical creatures include early gulls, herons, and ducks, and large marine reptiles, including flippered lizards.

a Plants
b Invertebrates
c Fishes
d Reptiles
e Birds
f Mammals

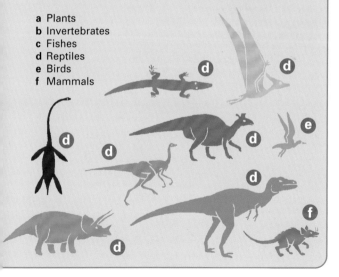

The Paleocene Epoch

The Paleocene ("old recent life")
Epoch is the first of the Early
Tertiary (third) Period,
occupying most of the
Cenozoic Era, the "age of
recent life." Retreating seas
expose dry land in much of
North America, Africa, and
Australia. South America is cut
adrift from North America, with its own unique
ark of animals.

New kinds of mammal are appearing everywhere,
including the first hoofed herbivores, rodents,
and squirrel-like primates. Carnivorous mammals
meet competition from big flightless birds of
prey. At sea, gastropods and bivalves replace
ammonites as the leading molluscs. Sharks are
plentiful.

65–54 million years ago

a Invertebrates
b "Amphibians"
c Mammals

The Eocene Epoch

The Eocene or "dawn of recent life" Epoch is generally warm and mild—tropical palms flourish in such unlikely places as London!—with seas flooding much of Africa, Australia, and Siberia. India and Africa are isolated island continents, while Australia breaks away from Antarctica. Huge lava flows leak out of great fissures in the Earth's surface. Mammals flourish during this period, with the

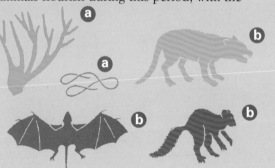

54–38 million years ago

first sea cows and whales swimming in the seas.
Rodents prosper as the main small mammals and
insectivores give rise to bats. Primates include the
ancestors of today's lemurs and tarsiers.

a Invertebrates
b Mammals
c Birds

The Oligocene Epoch

The Oligocene ("few recent" kinds of life) Epoch sees South America finally separate from Antarctica, allowing ocean currents to circulate round the southernmost continent for the first time. The Antarctic ice cap now begins to form, cooling the climate. As a result, grasses and temperate trees replace tropical vegetation in many areas.

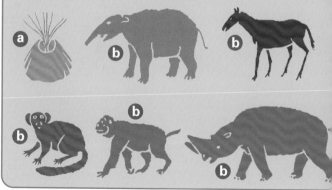

36–26 million years ago

Grazing and browsing mammals, such as horses, camels, and rhinoceroses flourish on the grasslands, while brontotheres range over North America and Asia. Dogs, cats, stoats, pigs, and ratlike rodents increase in numbers. At sea, the early whales die out and are largely replaced by toothed whales.

a Invertebrates
b Mammals
c Birds

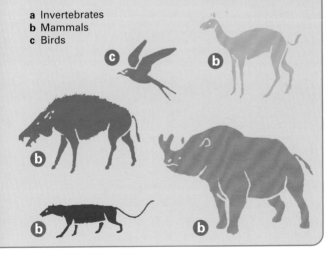

The Miocene Epoch

The Miocene or "less recent" Epoch, with fewer modern creatures than the next epoch, is the longest of the seven epochs, and the first of the Late Tertiary Period, which continues to the present day. Ice covers Antarctica, India crashes into Asia, causing the Himalayas to rise, while Africa is now connected to Eurasia.

27–7 million years ago

As grasslands spread around the world, the variety of mammals becomes ever richer. Many are hoofed grazers and browsers, including horses, rhinoceroses, early deer, and giraffes, and many different primates. Armadillos, anteaters, and horselike Litopterns evolve in isolated South America.

a Plants
b Mammals
c Birds

The Pliocene Epoch

The Pliocene ("more recent") Epoch ends the lengthy Tertiary Period of the Cenozoic Era. The continents have taken up their present-day positions and land now links North and South America, allowing animals to move from one continent to the other. Ice caps cool lands and oceans in the polar regions.

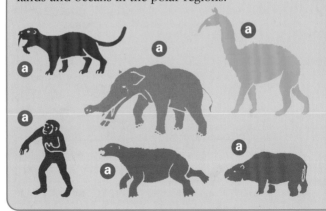

7–2 million years ago

As grasslands replace forests, grazing mammals spread at the expense of browsers. Cattle, sheep, gazelles, and other bovids thrive. Early elephants, antelopes, and the ancestors of humankind roam Africa. Rodents float on mats of vegetation south from Indonesia to colonize Australia.

a Mammals
b Birds

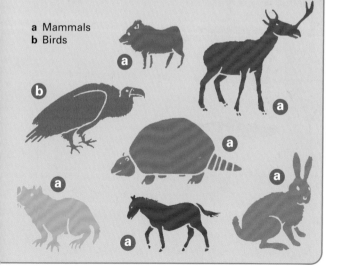

The Pleistocene Epoch

During the Pleistocene ("most recent") Epoch, huge ice sheets cover northern North America, Europe, and Asia. Southern South America, Australia, New Zealand, and Antarctica are also icier than they are today. Sea levels are about 330 feet (100 m) lower than

2 million–10,000 years ago

the present day, creating dry land bridges between North America and Asia, and New Guinea and Australia.

a Mammals
b Birds

2. Life in the Sea

LIFE BEGINS IN THE SEA

Life as we know it today—humans, animals, birds, fish, reptiles, insects, plants, fungi, and the rest—all began in the sea. More than 3.8 billion years ago, tiny one-celled organisms developed in the oceans, a vast, chemical-rich test tube shrouded by volcanic gases and intensively bombarded by solar radiation and electric storms.

Quite how this happened we do not know, but perhaps lightning and ultraviolet radiation acting on simple chemicals created compounds of amino

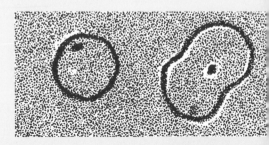

acids. These compounds then created simple, one-celled organisms called bacteria.

Much later, more developed bacteria contained the green pigment chlorophyll, enabling them to use the energy in sunshine to build their own food compounds from carbon dioxide and water. This process of photosynthesis yielded free oxygen as waste. In time, this oxygen shielded the Earth's surface from harmful ultraviolet rays and formed a rich new source of energy. By about 1 billion years ago, as the fossils below show, these one-celled organisms were able to divide and multiply, ultimately producing far more complex life forms.

Early complex cells

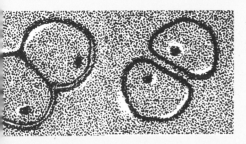

Food for life

About 1.2 billion years ago, simple one-celled organisms had developed enough to swallow cyanobacteria or "blue-green algae" and other bacteria that then lived on inside them, producing the food to enable them to survive. These protists, as they are called, reproduced by dividing, like bacteria, but most of their ingredients also split, in increasingly complex ways. Prehistoric protists—shown vastly magnified here—drifted around in the sea, living and dying in their millions to be preserved eventually as fossils.

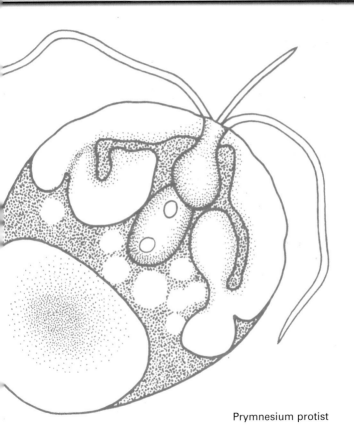

Prymnesium protist

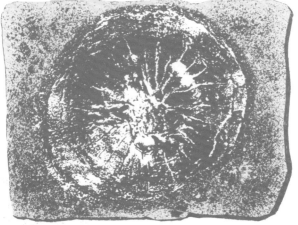

Fossilized jellyfish

With or without protection

Early life forms that developed under the sea came in two basic types. Coelenterates, or "hollow-gutted animals" (above left), were mostly jellylike creatures and consisted of many cells organized to produce a central body cavity with a mouth surrounded by tentacles and stinging cells

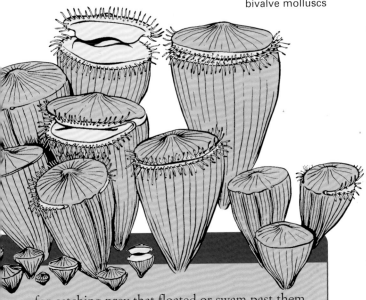

Colony of rudist
bivalve molluscs

for catching prey that floated or swam past them.
Molluscs or "soft animals" (above right) had a
shell or muscular foot and a digestive tract. They
grazed on algae, filter food particles from mud or
water, or hunt for food.

First sea life

We are not very sure what the first sea creatures looked like, because they had soft bodies and so quickly decayed after death, leaving no fossil record. Unusually, some creatures dating back to the Precambrian period 560 million years ago have been found fossilized in rock in Ediacara, Australia. Here they lived in a shallow sea and were preserved in the soft beach sand.

Hundreds of specimens exist, some of which are very detailed. Unfortunately, most are so different from creatures alive today that it is difficult to understand what they were and how they lived. But some of them are recognizable as primitive jellyfish, sponges, worms, and sea anemones, as well as the soft corals we call sea pens.

a Early jellyfish
b Sea pen
c Spriggina
d Dickinsonia
e Tube-worm
f Sea anemone

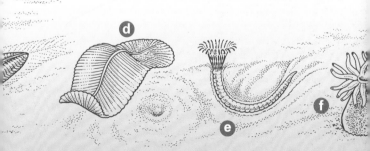

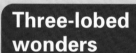

Three-lobed wonders

Trilobites—the word means "three-lobed"—
were a primitive type of arthropod, an invertebrate
with a segmented body and a hard (outer)
exoskeleton. At least 15,000 different species of
trilobites lived in shallow seas during the Paleozoic
Era (543–248 mya) and ranged from less than

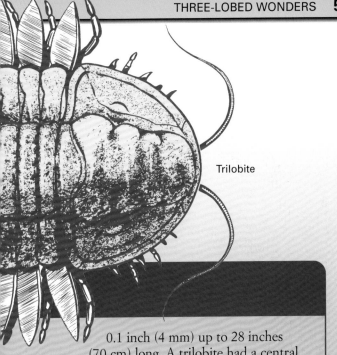

Trilobite

0.1 inch (4 mm) up to 28 inches (70 cm) long. A trilobite had a central raised ridge along its back flanked by two flattish side lobes, each divided into many segments from which spouted a pair of limbs designed for walking, swimming, breathings, and handling food.

Life in a shell

During the Cambrian Period (543–490 mya), creatures began to develop hard skeletons or shells that gave them a new means of protection. These also provided something for muscles to attach themselves to, allowing new ways of moving and feeding. The nautilus, a type of mollusc,

Nautilus

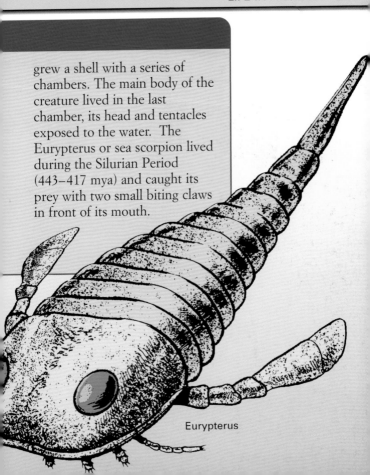

grew a shell with a series of chambers. The main body of the creature lived in the last chamber, its head and tentacles exposed to the water. The Eurypterus or sea scorpion lived during the Silurian Period (443–417 mya) and caught its prey with two small biting claws in front of its mouth.

Eurypterus

Life on the reef

The first reefs appeared during the Cambrian Period (543–490 mya), built by primitive sponges with supporting calcium carbonate skeletons. Over the years, these slowly piled up to form a solid reef several yards thick. This simple reef provided a home where other animals could live. By the Silurian Period (443–417 mya), reef-building was at its peak. Primitive corals formed branching groups that helped build the reef, while other coral types formed big colonies with fan-shaped or chain-like skeletons. The reef was home to crinoids or sea lilies, as well as trilobites and nautiloids, early relatives of the squid.

a Crinoids
b Sponges
c Trilobite
d Straight-shelled
e Nautiloid
f Corals

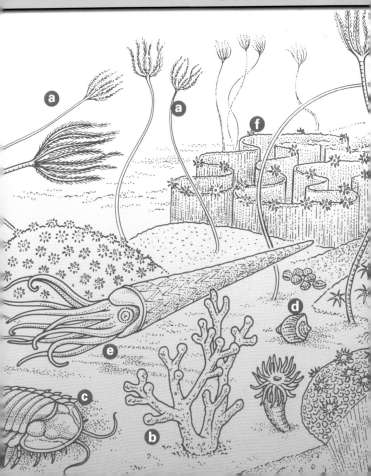

Jaws

Placoderms—the name means "plated skins"—
swam in the seas from about 440 to 355 million
years ago. Their skins were heavily armored with
bone and were powerful swimmers, with two
pairs of side fins and a strong tail. Placoderms
came in many different shapes and sizes, some
looking like modern fish but others growing to
enormous sizes: the Dunkleosteus grew up to
33 feet (10 m) longer than modern day great
white shark. Its head was joined and the top jaw
swung up, the lower jaw down, revealing a giant
cavity with massive teeth that quickly consume
any likely prey.

Placoderm

Dunkleosteus

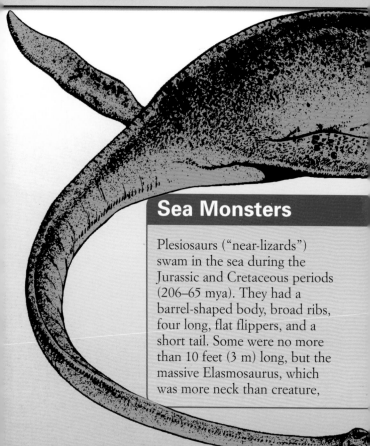

Sea Monsters

Plesiosaurs ("near-lizards") swam in the sea during the Jurassic and Cretaceous periods (206–65 mya). They had a barrel-shaped body, broad ribs, four long, flat flippers, and a short tail. Some were no more than 10 feet (3 m) long, but the massive Elasmosaurus, which was more neck than creature,

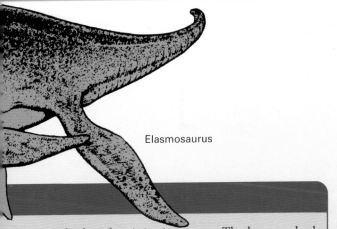

Elasmosaurus

stretched 39 feet (12 m) or more. The long-necked plesiosaurs lived at or near the surface and were expert fishers, while their short-necked cousins dived to the bottom to feed on ammonites. Both shared the seas with ichthyosaurs ("fish lizards"), aquatic reptiles with fins, flippers, long narrow jaws, and a superbly streamlined body. Some grew up to 75 feet (23 m) long, but the smaller versions looked much like modern day dolphins.

Tylosaurus

Sea Lizards

The first lizards appeared on land about 230 million years ago. Some eventually developed strange aquatic forms, such as mosasaurs, during the late Cretaceous Period (144–65 mya). These huge creatures, like the Tylosaurus show here, grew up to 26 feet (8 m) long. They swam in the shallow seas, seizing fish, reptiles, and plesiosaurs in their sharp-toothed jaws. Because of their size and specialization for life in water, it is unlikely later mosasaurs could move on land. Mosasaur relatives, the dolichosaurs, probably gave rise to the modern snake family.

Cleaning up the seabed

The first reptiles to take to the water were the mesosaurs, nearly 300 million years ago. Mesosaurs lived in fresh water and either caught fish or strained small creatures from the water to eat. They grew up to 3 feet (1 m) long, had large, powerful hind legs, and long flat tails to propel them along. Their successors, the placodonts, lived in seawater and had forward-pointing, peg-like teeth, which they used to pluck shellfish and molluscs from the sea floor. The placodonts, which lived in the Triassic Period (248–206 mya), grew up to 6 feet (2 m) long, but because they were so bulky, they were probably slow swimmers.

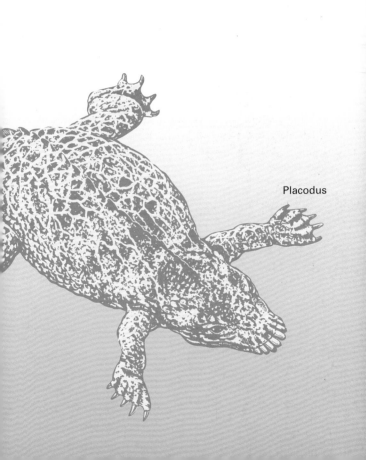

Placodus

Living in water and on land

Some prehistoric creatures managed the clever feat to live both underwater and on land. The lungfish, three types of which survive today, date back to 350 million years ago and have gills to breathe underwater and lungs to breathe air on land, useful during the dry season when its lakes and ponds dry up. Other ancient fish, such as the Eusthenopteron, developed paired fins with bones similar to a human leg, helping them to walk on land for short distances. The modern day Mexican Axolotl still has legs, although it is totally aquatic.

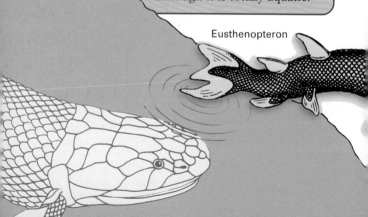

Eusthenopteron

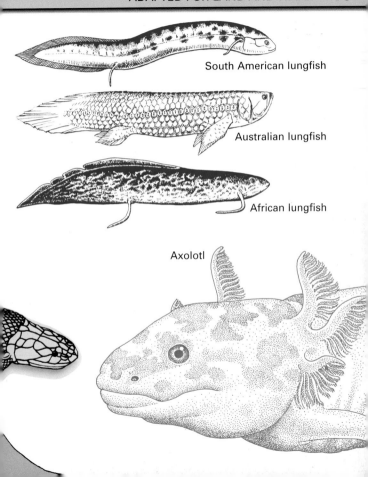

South American lungfish

Australian lungfish

African lungfish

Axolotl

Back from the dead

In 1938 fishermen off the coast of South Africa trawled up the strangest fish they had ever seen. It was 5 feet (1.5 m) long, weighed 180 pounds (80 kg), and was bluish in color. Scientists quickly realized that this fish was in the fact the prehistoric coelacanth, known to have existed more than 350 million years ago but last found

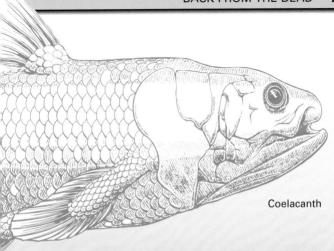

Coelacanth

fossilized in rocks about 70 million years old. The modern day coelacanth lives around the Comoros Islands between Madagascar and East Africa and is found at depths of 500–1,000 feet (150–300 m), where its eyes can operate in the very dim light. It produces live young, and feeds on a variety of small fish and squids.

3. Life on the Land

OUT OF THE WATER

In the beginning, more than 3.8 billion years ago, tiny, one-celled organisms developed in the sea. A billion years ago, these one-celled organisms were able to divide and multiply, producing far more complex life forms. Jellyfish and other soft-bodied creatures floated round in the sea 560 million years ago, and were joined by jawless fish 30 or so million

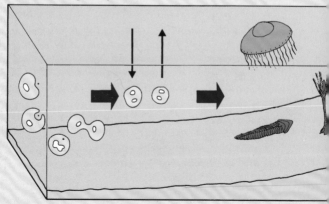

From one-celled organisms
to land-walking tetrapods

years later. The big breakthrough came about 360 million years ago. Then a vertebrate fish with lungs crawled ashore on stubby fins that had evolved as limbs and continued to breathe and live on dry land. These limb-bearing vertebrates are known as tetrapods, meaning "four feet," and are the ancestors of reptiles and dinosaurs.

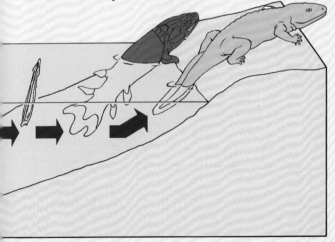

The first plants

Plants with internal channels for transporting water and other liquids are known as vascular plants and include ferns, conifers, and flowering plants. The first upright vascular plant, the cooksonia, probably appeared about 420 million years ago, during the Silurian Period (435–410 mya), and had simple, forked, leafless stems, each ending in a spore-filled cap. Later arrivals during the Carboniferous Period (355–295 mya) include the giant lepidodendron club moss, which grew up to 100 feet (30 m), and the calamites horsetail. Over the millennia, as leaves dropped and the trees died, layers of vegetation were compressed under rocks to form thick bands of coal. Flowering plants evolved about 120 millions years ago, during the Cretaceous Period (144–65 mya).

Evolution of a leaf

a Branching stems with broad, flat rims

b Branching stems increase and move closer together

c Wide-rimmed branches fuse together to form leaves

d Lepidodendron a form of giant moss that grows to 100 ft (30 m)

e Calamites jointed stems-like palm trees grew to 100 ft (30 m)

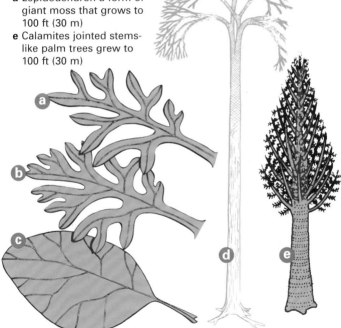

First steps

Scientists are unsure whether tetrapods developed limbs so that they could crawl ashore and search for food or new habitats, or whether the limbs were formed to help their owners clamber through aquatic plants. It seems unlikely that ichthyostega, who lived during the Devonian Period (417–354 mya) ever left the water to stand like on all fours, as its hind limbs look so flipperlike and its tail is more like a fin. The later mastodon lizard, from the Triassic Period (248–206 mya) probably spent all his life in the water too, coming ashore just to seize its unwary prey before taking back to its watery lair.

Ichthyostega

Mastodonsaurus

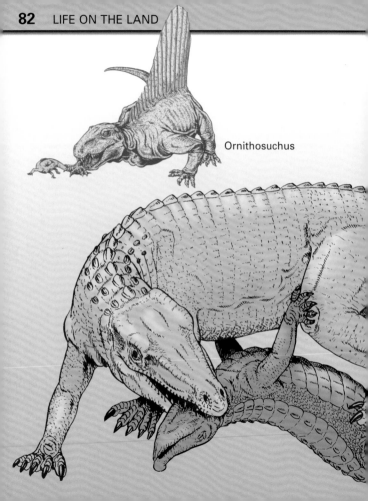

Ornithosuchus

Reptiles on land

During the late Permian Period (290–248 mya), a group of reptiles evolved known as archosaurs. These later split into two main groups: ornithodirans, which includes dinosaurs and birds, and crocodylotarsians, the ancestors of today's crocodiles. Crocodylotarsians had ankle-joints that allowed them to twist their feet to the side when walking, hence their name, which means "crocodile ankle." Some of these beasts, like the ornithosuchus, were up to 13 feet (4 m) long, and had much longer hind legs than arms.

The Age of Dinosaurs

Dinosaurs stalked the Earth during the Mesozoic Era (248–65 mya), the "Age of Dinosaurs." The first dinosaurs were probably two-legged hunters no bigger than a dog, but they soon evolved into a bewildering and terrifying variety of shapes and sizes, some as big and as heavy as a house, others no bigger than a hen. No individual dinosaur species lasted longer than a few million years, but as one species died out, another came to take its place. Scientists have identified at least 900 different types, but there are probably many more waiting to be discovered in the fossil record.

The first insects

The first known insects were tiny, wingless arthropods— that is, invertebrates with segmented bodies and a hard (outer) exoskeleton—that lived in the Devonian Period (417–354 mya). By about 320 mya, some insects had developed wings. We know a lot about early insects because many of them were trapped in

Spider trapped in sticky tree sap

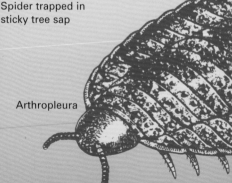

Arthropleura

the resinous sap of conifers that has since hardened into amber. Some ancient insects grew to huge lengths: the arthropleura millipede, which munched rotting vegetation on Carboniferous forest floors 300 million years ago, grew up to 6 feet (1.8 m) long.

Spider preserved in hardened amber

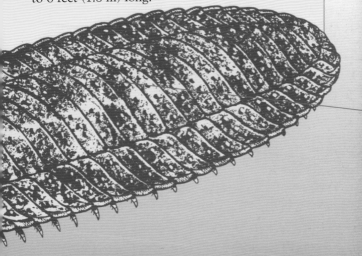

The first mammals

Mammals evolved from a group of scaly, cold-blooded reptiles known as synapsids ("with arch") because they had a large hole low in the skull behind each eye through which passed muscles that worked the jaw. Synapsids lived in the Permian Period (290–248 mya); over the next 50 million years, a sub-group of synapsids called therapsids ("mammal arches") evolved. Some of

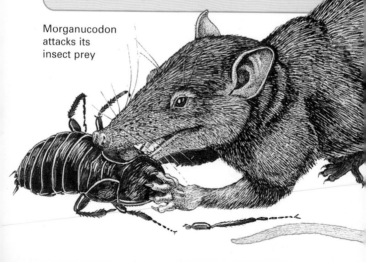

Morganucodon attacks its insect prey

these, such as the cynognathus, were warm-blooded and had a furry coat. From these the first mammals evolved during the Jurassic Period (203–135 mya). These were probably tiny, shrew-like creatures, such as the morganucodon, which shared many of the same teeth and bone structure as their modern day relations.

Cynognathus

The mammal ancestors

Some of the mammals we are familiar with today have evolved from giants that lived during the Eocene Epoch about 35 million years ago. The aepycamelus was actually a prehistoric camel but looks more like a giraffe, as it stood 10 feet (3 m) tall, enabling it to browse on leafy twigs high off the ground. The indricotherium, the largest land mammal ever known, is the ancestor of our rhinoceros. Its shoulders were 15 feet (4.6 m) off the ground, but you are unlikely to meet one today, as it died out 20 million years ago.

Aepycamelus

Indricotherium

Animals eat animals

Many of the early mammals were herbivores, but they were easy prey for the carnivores that dominated the mammal kingdom from the Tertiary Period (65–1.8 mya) onwards. There are two main types of carnivore: the feliforms, including cats, civets, hyenas, and mongooses—and the caniforms, including dogs, weasels, racoons, pandas, bears, seals, and walruses. Both types are skilled at hunting and killing, making herbivores like the ground sloth an easy target for a quick-witted, agile smilodon.

Smilodon attacking
a mylodon

4. Life in the Air

The biggest flier of all time was the pterodactyl Quetzalcoatlus, named after the Mexican god Quetzalcoatl, who took the form of a feathered snake. It weighed about 180 pounds (15 kg) and had a wingspan of at least 33 feet (12 m), perhaps even reaching 39 feet (15 m). Because its weight was low compared with its wing area, it could soar at low speeds for long distances on the air thermals without flapping its wings. It probably fed on fish, dipping its toothless beak in the seas and rivers to catch them, while flying slowly across water.

Quetzalcoatlus

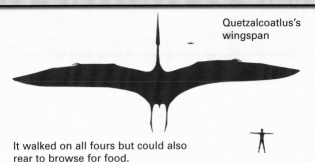

Quetzalcoatlus's wingspan

It walked on all fours but could also rear to browse for food.

Other fliers

Quetzalcoatlus lived during the Cretaceous Period (144–65 mya), but it was insects that first took off during the Carboniferous Period (354–290 mya). The oldest known bird dinosaur, archaeopteryx, flew during the Jurassic Period (206–144 mya). During the Tertiary Period (65–1.8 mya), descendants of bird dinosaurs evolved into the flyers we see today.

Insects

In the late Carboniferous Period 300 million years ago, primitive dragonflies with a wingspan of 28 inches (70 cm), and a body to match, flew through the swamps. Each of its four wings had a separate pair of muscles acting directly on each wing, one muscle to raise a wing, the other to lower it. This meant the two pairs of wings did not have a synchronized beat, but they still enabled the dragonfly to hover, fly fast, and catch and eat its insect prey.

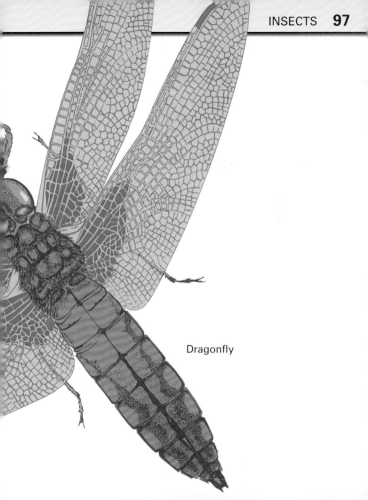

Dragonfly

Gliding reptiles

The fossil record shows that almost as long as there have been lizardlike reptiles, some have taken to the air by gliding. The first of these, including Icarosaurus, lived during the Triassic Period (248–206 mya). It climbed trees with its long struts folded back. As it dived off into the air, its struts swung forward, opening skin parachutes.

Coelurosauravus

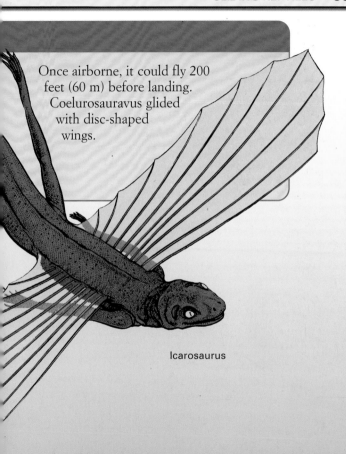

Once airborne, it could fly 200
feet (60 m) before landing.
Coelurosauravus glided
with disc-shaped
wings.

Icarosaurus

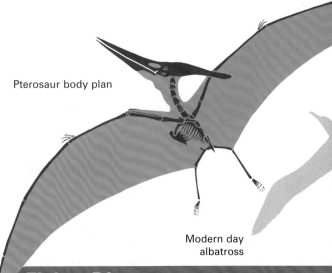

Pterosaur body plan

Modern day albatross

Flying Dinosaurs

Pterosaurs ("winged lizards") included the first and largest flying backboned creatures. Thought to be a close kin of the dinosaur, they evolved from the gliding reptiles during the Jurassic Period (206–144 mya) and died out at the end of

Pteranadon launches into the
winds that blew on sea cliffs

the Cretaceous Period 65 million years ago. A
typical pterosaur had skin wings stretched
between the limbs and body, a light but strong
skeleton, and well-developed powers of sight and
wing control.

Hanging about

There are some 70 known kinds of pterosaur, and probably many more that have yet to be discovered, ranging in size from some no bigger than a modern blackbird to the giant Quetzalcoatlus. They could walk on all four limbs and could possibly run on their two hind legs. Their three fingers on the front of the wing had sharp claws, suggesting they climbed well, and some could probably hang from trees or cliffs by their hind legs.

Pterodactylus on all fours

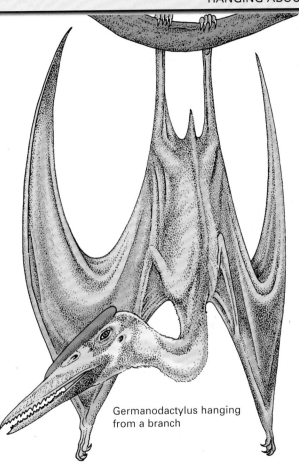

Germanodactylus hanging
from a branch

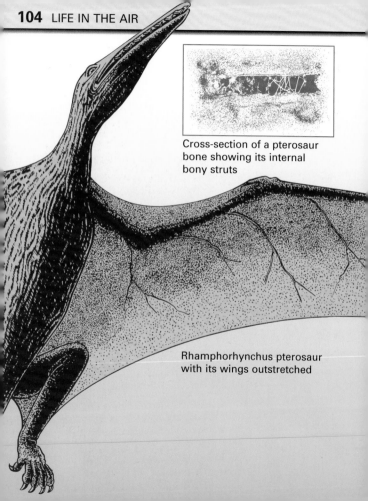

Cross-section of a pterosaur bone showing its internal bony struts

Rhamphorhynchus pterosaur with its wings outstretched

Bone and muscle

Pterosaurs had a remarkable set of fingers halfway along its wing. Three of them were small and had claws that could be used for grasping or clutching. The fourth finger stretched along the rest of the wing to its tip, keeping the wing outstretched. The wing itself was made of leathery skin with strengthening fibers and only the fourth finger to support it. The muscles that worked its wings were in the upper part of the arm and ran down to the breastbone in its body. As in modern day birds, the breastbone was large enough to fit these muscles.

Bringing up kids

Dinosaur birds, like all reptiles, hatched hard-shelled eggs, which they then protected in a nest until the embryos were ready to break through the shell as young chicks. The nests were hollowed-out dips in the ground and thus vulnerable to attack, so both parents looked after the eggs and protected them against all predators. By day, the soft downy feathers of a parent's wing shielded the eggs from the sun's heat and from wind-blown sand, while at night, heat from its body kept the eggs warm. Once hatched, the chicks would use their claws to explore and climb trees before they were ready to fly.

Modern day hoatzin
with claws on its wings

Citipati on
the nest

Beaks with teeth

Gallodactylus

Pterodactyls probably evolved from long-tailed pterosaurs during the late Jurassic Period (206–144 mya). Their lack of a stabilizing tail suggests that they had a highly developed nervous system to control their flight. Their heads were set at an angle to the backbone, as birds' heads are today, and they had elongated jaws. In some, the teeth were very specialized, in others, absent altogether. A typical pterodactyl jaw had teeth adapted to a fish diet.

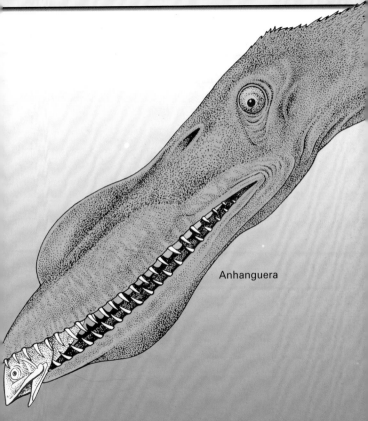

Anhanguera

a Archaeopteryx
b Phorusrhacus
  longissimus
c Gastornis
d Dinornis
  giganteus
e Aepyornis
  maximus
f Modern day
  chicken

Grounded birds

Some experts think that the first known flying bird, archaeopteryx ("ancient wing"), climbed trees and fluttered down to the ground, while others believe it took off by sprinting into a headwind. But not all birds could fly. Phorusrhacus longissimus stood 6 feet 6 inches (2 m) tall and devoured goat-sized creatures with its huge beak. Gastornis ("terror crane") was the same size but far older, living about 50 million years ago. Aepyornis maximus ("greatest of the high birds") lived in Madagascar and was the heaviest bird ever, weighing in at a vast 970 pounds (440 kg.) It only died out in about 1700 CE. Dinornis giganteus ("giant terrible bird"), the New Zealand moa, was the tallest known bird, standing 11 feet 6 inches (3.5 m) tall. It died out about much the same time.

5. Invertebrates

ABOUT INVERTEBRATES

Invertebrates (animals without a backbone) are mostly small, soft-bodied creatures, although many have a hard outer casing. They account for all but one major animal group or phylum. Almost all of the invertebrates, more than 20 phyla, appeared at least 500 million years ago. Many of these phyla, though, contain animals such as worms and jellyfish that left poor fossil records.

The 11 prehistoric creatures described in this chapter come from five invertebrate phyla. Mollusca (molluscs) (**1**) includes clams, snails, squid, and the extinct ammonites. Onychophora (**2**) features "rubber-legged" velvet worms still found in tropical forests. Arthropoda (arthropods) (**3**), or jointed-legged animals, includes insects, spiders, millipedes, crabs, and the long-extinct trilobites. Echinodermata (echinoderms) (**4**) comprises the spiny-skinned sea urchins, starfishes, sea cucumbers, and their relatives. Hemichordata (hemichordates) (**5**) includes tiny wormlike creatures called graptolites that built tube-shaped homes important as fossils.

Hemichordates and echinoderms are invertebrates closely related to the phylum Chordata (chordates) (**6**), the great group containing all the creatures shown in chapters 3 to 7.

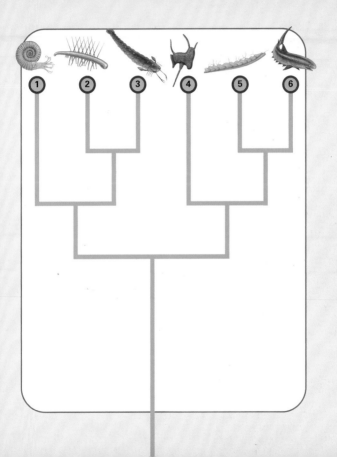

SPRIGGINA

Spriggina is one of the earliest known animals: a puzzling little leaf-shaped creature that lived on a shallow sea floor more than 550 million years ago.

The first scientist to study its fossils thought that it had a blunt head, a long body divided in segments, and a tapering tail. He decided that *Spriggina* was a worm that crawled on the sea floor, feeding on edible scraps.

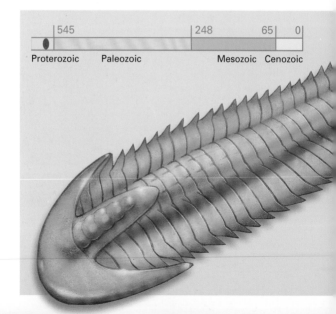

	545		248	65	0
Proterozoic		Paleozoic		Mesozoic	Cenozoic

Another scientist thought *Spriggina* grew on the seabed, fastened by what looks like its head, a bit like a seaweed or the creatures called crinoids or sea-lilies. This scientist believed this was one of several strange, flat, "quilted" creatures unlike any alive today.

The third, and perhaps likeliest, possibility is that this animal was some kind of primitive pre-arthropod or arthropod related to such joint-legged creatures as today's crabs and spiders, insects, scorpions and mites.

Name	*Spriggina*
Pronunciation	sprig-EE-na
Meaning	"Little Sprigg"
Phylum	Arthropoda?
Class	Unclassified
Order	Unclassified
Length	1.8 in (4.5 cm)
Food	Edible scraps?
Location	Southern Australia
Aeon	Proterozoic (550–560 mya)

HALLUCIGENIA

The scientist who named *Hallucigenia* had never seen anything like this small fossil creature. The little worm-like beast seemed to have walked around on seven pairs of long spiky stilts. Seven pairs of wriggly tentacles sprouted from its back. No wonder the scientist gave it a name suggesting a beast dreamed up in a nightmare.

Later, another scientist realized that *Hallucigenia* had been described upside down. Its stiltlike "legs" were rows of

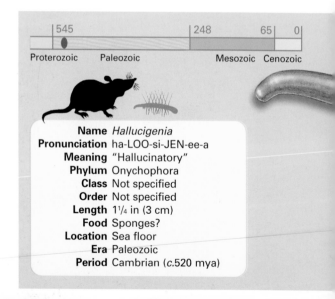

Name	*Hallucigenia*
Pronunciation	ha-LOO-si-JEN-ee-a
Meaning	"Hallucinatory"
Phylum	Onychophora
Class	Not specified
Order	Not specified
Length	1¼ in (3 cm)
Food	Sponges?
Location	Sea floor
Era	Paleozoic
Period	Cambrian (*c.*520 mya)

545   248   65   0
Proterozoic   Paleozoic   Mesozoic   Cenozoic

protective spikes sticking up from its back. Its real legs were the long, fleshy "tentacles."

Hallucigenia was probably an ancient relative of the so-called velvet worms that creep about on small rubbery legs on the floors of moist tropical forests. Unlike velvet worms, *Hallucigenia* lived on the floor of the sea. Perhaps it crawled over sponges and ate them, like *Aysheaia*, another wormlike creature with legs.

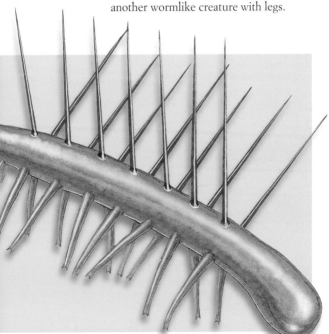

ANOMALOCARIS

This weird sea beast was the earliest known large carnivorous creature. After death it broke up into bits, and, when their fossils were discovered, scientists at first believed they came from three different animals, so gave them different names.

Anomalocaris swam by waving up and down the flaps sticking out from its sides, much as squid swim today. Big eyes helped it to spot prey crawling on the seabed.

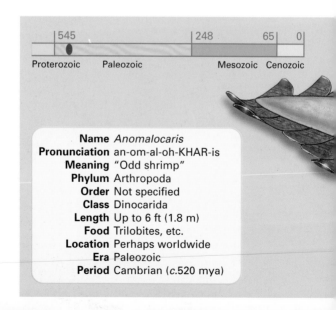

545		248	65	0
Proterozoic	Paleozoic		Mesozoic	Cenozoic

Name	*Anomalocaris*
Pronunciation	an-om-al-oh-KHAR-is
Meaning	"Odd shrimp"
Phylum	Arthropoda
Order	Not specified
Class	Dinocarida
Length	Up to 6 ft (1.8 m)
Food	Trilobites, etc.
Location	Perhaps worldwide
Era	Paleozoic
Period	Cambrian (c.520 mya)

Anomalocaris would have gripped small, hard-shelled sea creatures with its shrimplike front limbs. These then pulled its victim to the round open mouth under its head. Around this mouth ran a ring of sharp teeth strong enough to crack open a trilobite's hard body covering.

Scientists believe that *Anomalocaris* was an early, primitive kind of arthropod. Living arthropods include the crabs, insects, and spiders.

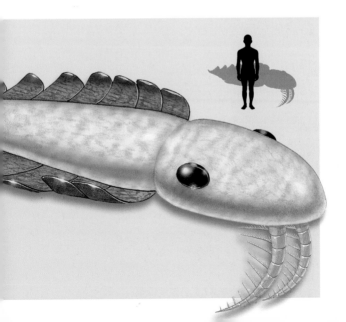

CALYMENE

Calymene looked like a woodlouse but lived under the sea. It was a trilobite, one of a great extinct group of arthropods named after their three-lobed bodies with a ridge down the middle and a lobe on each side.

Calymene's head shield had bulging many-lensed eyes like an insect's. Behind the head was an armored thorax of segments, each with its own legs and feathery gills. There was a short stubby tail shield, called a pygidium.

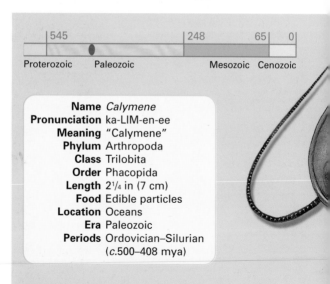

545		248	65	0
Proterozoic	Paleozoic		Mesozoic	Cenozoic

Name	*Calymene*
Pronunciation	ka-LIM-en-ee
Meaning	"Calymene"
Phylum	Arthropoda
Class	Trilobita
Order	Phacopida
Length	2¼ in (7 cm)
Food	Edible particles
Location	Oceans
Era	Paleozoic
Periods	Ordovician–Silurian (*c*.500–408 mya)

As *Calymene* scurried about on the seabed, tiny spines on its legs pushed scraps of food forward under its body along a groove to its mouth.

If something scared it, this trilobite rolled up in a tight little armored ball. It outgrew its armor now and then. Each time, the old coat split and fell off. Underneath was a new, soft suit of armor that quickly hardened.

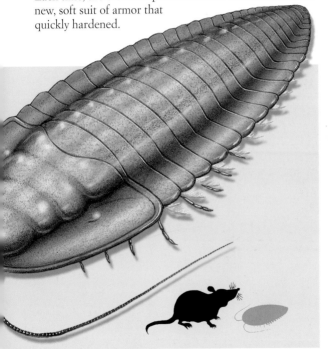

ARTHROPLEURA

Imagine meeting a millipede the length of a man and as wide as a boot is long. Such monsters were the largest arthropods that ever lived out of water. Two grooves down their backs divided these so-called arthropleurids in three lengthwise, rather like trilobites. Indeed, people once supposed that arthropleurids had been trilobites living on land instead of under the sea.

Arthropleura swarmed over moist forest floors like a

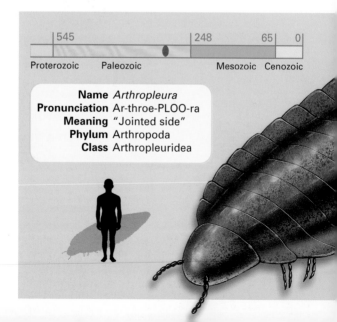

| 545 | 248 | 65 | 0 |

Proterozoic   Paleozoic   Mesozoic Cenozoic

Name *Arthropleura*
Pronunciation Ar-throe-PLOO-ra
Meaning "Jointed side"
Phylum Arthropoda
Class Arthropleuridea

miniature train, not on wheels but on up to 60 small, bristly legs that left marks like little tank tracks.

Scientists think that *Arthropleura* fed as it ploughed through the forest floor's carpet of mosses and dead leaves, much as millipedes do today. As it traveled it munched the club mosses that grew and died under the tall forest trees. We know this because one fossil specimen's gut was full of swallowed club mosses.

Order	Unclassified
Length	6 ft (1.8 m)
Food	Plant material
Location	Tropical forests
Era	Paleozoic
Period	Carboniferous (*c.*300 mya)

PTERYGOTUS

Longer than a man, this nightmarish beast without a
backbone was in its time the terror of the seas.

Six pairs of limbs sprouted from the broad, blunt head of
this giant "sea scorpion." The front pair formed long
"biting" claws. Next came four pairs of legs for crawling
along the seabed, then two long, wide paddles for
swimming slowly along. *Pterygotus* had no limbs on the
twelve segments of its long, tapered body, but by wagging

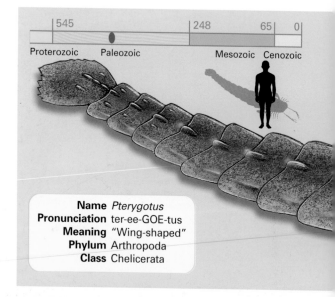

	545	248	65	0
Proterozoic	Paleozoic		Mesozoic	Cenozoic

Name	*Pterygotus*
Pronunciation	ter-ee-GOE-tus
Meaning	"Wing-shaped"
Phylum	Arthropoda
Class	Chelicerata

its broad, flat tail up and down it could make a sudden dash through the water to capture a victim.

The monster cruised slowly through the shallow seas off river mouths. Its large eyes were always watching for other creatures crawling on the seabed or swimming just above it. Suddenly its long, spiny claws would flash out to snatch up a slow-moving jawless fish, a trilobite, or a "sea scorpion" like itself but much smaller.

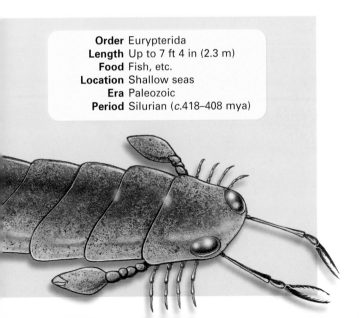

Order	Eurypterida
Length	Up to 7 ft 4 in (2.3 m)
Food	Fish, etc.
Location	Shallow seas
Era	Paleozoic
Period	Silurian (*c.*418–408 mya)

MESOLIMULUS

A carapace curved like a horseshoe earned *Mesolimulus* and its relatives the name horseshoe crabs.

Like most crabs, *Mesolimulus* lived in the sea and crawled about on the seabed. Its nearest relations, though, were not crabs but spiders and scorpions.

Mesolimulus had a broad, rounded, springy, hard shield protecting its combined head and thorax. A smaller shield guarded its abdomen, which sprouted a long, sharp spiny

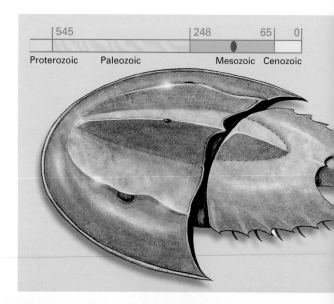

545		248	65	0
Proterozoic	Paleozoic		Mesozoic	Cenozoic

telson, or tail. On top of the main shield were small wide-set eyes. Concealed under its shields were the mouth, two small "biting claws," two pedipalps ("feelers"), eight walking legs, and gills.

Horseshoe crabs of one kind or another have been around for 300 million years. You can still see hordes of these living fossils swarming inshore at night to lay their eggs off the east coasts of North America and Asia.

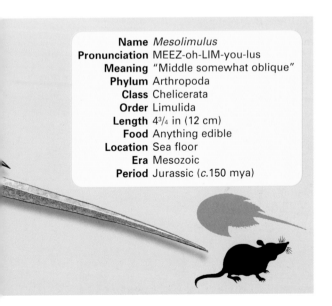

Name	*Mesolimulus*
Pronunciation	MEEZ-oh-LIM-you-lus
Meaning	"Middle somewhat oblique"
Phylum	Arthropoda
Class	Chelicerata
Order	Limulida
Length	4³/₄ in (12 cm)
Food	Anything edible
Location	Sea floor
Era	Mesozoic
Period	Jurassic (*c.*150 mya)

MEGANEURA

Nearly 150 million years before the first known bird flew, proto-dragonflies with the wingspan of hawks zoomed over hot, swampy forests.

Meganeura was among the largest of these gigantic invertebrates: a creature with a typical insect's three-part body: head, thorax, and abdomen. The swiveling head bore massive jaws and huge bulbous, multifaceted

eyes designed to spot anything moving. The thorax bore six legs and two pairs of long, narrow, transparent wings stiffened by a network of veins. The wings always stuck out sideways. *Meganeura* could not fold its wings back over its abdomen, as more advanced insects can.

Darting to and fro over sunlit glades, this fast, agile hunter zoomed in on clumsier fliers. Like living dragonflies, it probably used its long legs to grab these insects and bring them forward to its mouth.

Name *Meganeura*
Pronunciation meg-an-YOU-ra
Meaning "Big nerves"
Phylum Arthropoda
Class Insecta
Order Palaeoptera
Wingspan 27½ in (70 cm)
Food Flying insects
Location Tropical forests
Era Paleozoic
Period Carboniferous (*c.*295 mya)

545		248	65	0
Proterozoic	Paleozoic		Mesozoic	Cenozoic

PAVLOVIA

Pavlovia was a soft-bodied sea creature with tentacles at its head end, poking from a ribbed, flat-sided shell coiled like a ram's horn. It belonged to the ammonites, an extinct group of cephalopods: keen-eyed, large brained molluscs that include today's squid and octopuses.

Pavlovia was jet propelled, swimming backward by squirting water forward. When it seized prey in its tentacles these fed the food to jaws shaped like a beak.

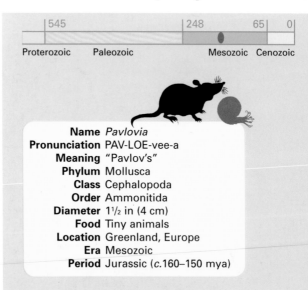

545	248	65	0
Proterozoic	Paleozoic	Mesozoic	Cenozoic

Name	*Pavlovia*
Pronunciation	PAV-LOE-vee-a
Meaning	"Pavlov's"
Phylum	Mollusca
Class	Cephalopoda
Order	Ammonitida
Diameter	1½ in (4 cm)
Food	Tiny animals
Location	Greenland, Europe
Era	Mesozoic
Period	Jurassic (*c.*160–150 mya)

As the ammonite grew, it added chambers to the end of its shell, living only in the biggest, outer ones. Partitions between chambers formed wavy suture lines where they met the outer shell. This reinforced it against high water pressure if the creature dived, perhaps to feed fairly deep in the sea. Like its living relative the pearly nautilus, *Pavlovia* sank by pumping water through a tube into its chambers, and filled them with gas to go up.

COTHURNOCYSTIS

Cothurnocystis was a weird, flat, lopsided little sea beast no longer than your hand. Starfishes and sea urchins are among its known relatives, yet one scientist suggested that creatures like this one could have been the remote ancestors of vertebrates: all animals with a backbone—even us. (Most scientists, however, believe this unlikely.)

Cothurnocystis looked like a tiny boot covered in hard limy plates, with a long tail jutting down from the sole.

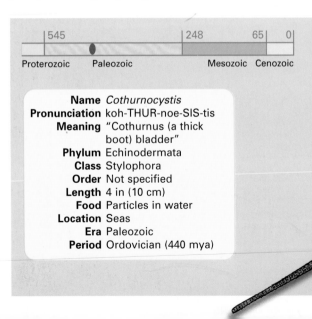

Name	*Cothurnocystis*
Pronunciation	koh-THUR-noe-SIS-tis
Meaning	"Cothurnus (a thick boot) bladder"
Phylum	Echinodermata
Class	Stylophora
Order	Not specified
Length	4 in (10 cm)
Food	Particles in water
Location	Seas
Era	Paleozoic
Period	Ordovician (440 mya)

Timeline: 545 — 248 — 65 — 0
Proterozoic | Paleozoic | Mesozoic | Cenozoic

Scientists had problems guessing how this strangely shaped animal worked. First they thought its tail was a stalk. Then they decided the creature lay flat and its tail dragged the boot over the muddy sea floor. Meanwhile, it could have sucked water into a hole corresponding to the place where a foot would slip into a boot. Tiny scraps of food in the water gave it nourishment. Then the used water could have squirted out through slits at the tiny boot's toe.

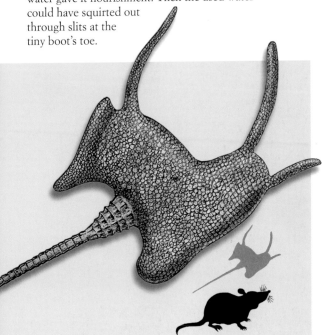

MONOGRAPTUS

Monograptus belonged to a group of creatures long known from puzzling fossils found in ancient rocks. They look like scribblings on stone, so scientists called them *graptolites* from Greek words meaning "writing on the rocks." They also look like tiny hacksaw blades.

Only the discovery of living fossil relatives showed what kind of creatures graptolites had been. They were colonies of tiny wormlike animals that lived in little cups—the

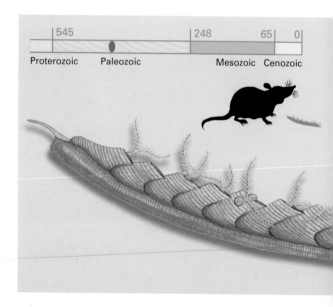

545		248	65	0
Proterozoic	Paleozoic		Mesozoic	Cenozoic

"teeth" along the "hacksaw blade." Each creature, called a zooid, built its cup as criss-crossed "bandages" made from a special protein. From this home the zooid poked out fleshy tentacles to grab tiny passing organisms as it drifted in the upper layers of the sea.

Monograptus zooids built a single "hacksaw blade," called more properly a *stipe*. Many graptolites had several stipes; some even branched out like a shrub.

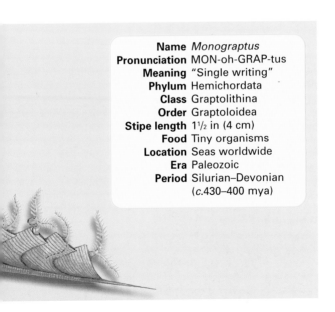

Name	*Monograptus*
Pronunciation	MON-oh-GRAP-tus
Meaning	"Single writing"
Phylum	Hemichordata
Class	Graptolithina
Order	Graptoloidea
Stipe length	1½ in (4 cm)
Food	Tiny organisms
Location	Seas worldwide
Era	Paleozoic
Period	Silurian–Devonian (*c.*430–400 mya)

6. Fishes

ABOUT FISHES

Fishes are cold-blooded water animals with a backbone, fins, and gills for breathing the oxygen in water. Paired muscles help them swim by waggling the body and its tail fin. Other fins help them brake and steer. Fishes and all other vertebrates (backboned animals) belong to the great group or phylum Chordata.

Fishes' chordate ancestors appeared more than 500 million years ago. Their nerve cord's swollen front end formed a brain, and from their springy notochord evolved the gristly backbone of early vertebrates.

Early vertebrates included possibly the eel-like Conodontia (1) ("cone-toothed" creatures) as well as jawless fishes such as the Heterostraci (2) ("different shells"). Such animals gave rise to fishes with jaws. Among these, the extinct Placodermi (3) ("plated fishes") and their relatives the sharks and other Chondrichthyes (4) ("cartilage fishes") had a gristly skeleton. The Acanthodii (5) known as "spiny sharks" had fins with bony spines, while the Osteichthyes (6) ("bony fishes") had skeletons of bone. Osteichthyans formed two major groups: the actinopterygians or "ray-finned" fishes such as *Leedsichthys* (7) with fins reinforced by bony rays, and the sarcopterygians or "flesh-finned" fishes such as *Panderichthys* (8) with fins that grew from fleshy lobes.

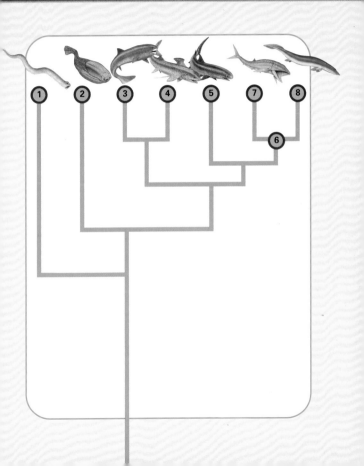

PROMISSUM

For more than 150 years, scientists puzzled over tiny fossils in ancient rocks that spanned 300 million years. They called them *conodonts* ("cone teeth"). Many looked like miniature combs with tall, sharp teeth.

In 1983 someone found the first fossil conodont animal, an eel like creature no longer than your fingernail. Later, people found a "giant." *Promissum*, 15¾ inches (40 cm) long, possessed a gaping mouth with rows of conodonts as

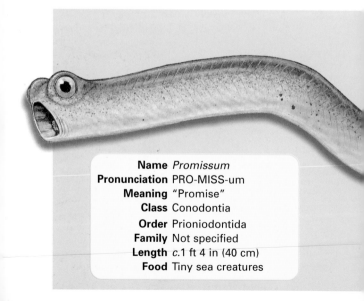

Name	*Promissum*
Pronunciation	PRO-MISS-um
Meaning	"Promise"
Class	Conodontia
Order	Prioniodontida
Family	Not specified
Length	*c.*1 ft 4 in (40 cm)
Food	Tiny sea creatures

tooth-bars in its throat, variously shaped for seizing, shearing, and grinding up its prey beneath the sea.

Conodonts lacked a braincase or spinal bones, but like true vertebrates had eyes, bone cells in the teeth, a rodlike notochord stiffening the body, and blocks of muscles powering sideways undulations as they swam. These hint that, more than 500 million years ago, conodonts were vertebrates related to the world's first fishes.

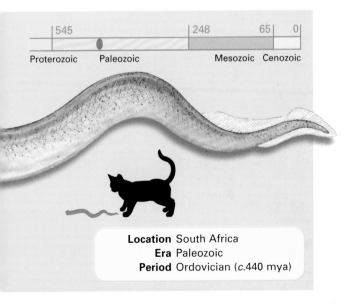

| 545 | | 248 | 65 | 0 |
| Proterozoic | Paleozoic | Mesozoic | Cenozoic |

Location South Africa
Era Paleozoic
Period Ordovician (*c.*440 mya)

SACABAMBASPIS

Sacabambaspis was a primitive, early fish with a gristly skeleton, no jaws, and no fins except on its tail. The body was a bit like a tadpole's. A shield of two big bony plates helped to protect its head and chest from large, hungry arthropods. Farther back, flexible scales covered its sides. *Sacabambaspis* swam by waggling its tail fin. Without fins to steer and brake it could not stop or turn.

Name	*Sacabambaspis*
Pronunciation	SAkka-bam-BAS-pis
Meaning	"Sacabamb[illa] shield"
Class	Agnatha
Order	Heterostraci
Family	Arandaspidae
Length	11¾ in (30 cm)
Food	Tiny organisms
Location	Shallow seas
Era	Paleozoic
Period	Ordovician (450 mya)

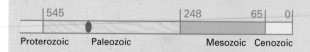

545		248	65	0
Proterozoic	Paleozoic		Mesozoic	Cenozoic

The mouth was just a small fixed hole below two eyes set at the very front of its blunt head, like tiny headlights on a miniature submarine. As it swam along it took in oxygen and particles of food with the water entering its open mouth. Breathed-out water, minus oxygen and food, left through tiny gill openings along the sides of its head.

Sacabambaspis lived in what was once a shallow sea, but its fossils were found near Sacabambilla, a Bolivian town in South America's high Andes Mountains.

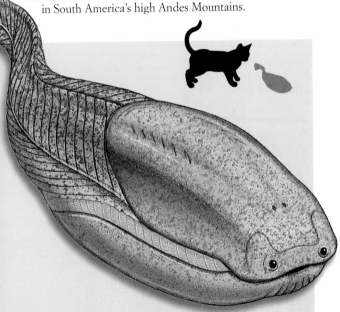

DUNKLEOSTEUS

This great ancient fish might have been one of the first animals to exceed 26 feet (8 m) long. It belonged to the *placoderms*, or "plated fishes," named after the bony plates protecting their bodies. Placoderms included some of the earliest fishes with jaws and paired fins.

Dunkleosteus looked rather sharklike. It had a huge, blunt, armored head and shoulder area, but the body farther

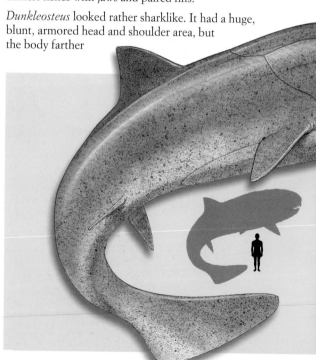

back lacked even ordinary scales. Together with its light, gristly skeleton this helped to cut down weight.

Despite its size, *Dunkleosteus* swam and turned fast enough to be a formidable big-game hunter. If a small shark unwisely came in range, *Dunkleosteus* rocked its head back on a set of ball and socket joints to make its jaws gape wide, revealing bony tooth plates sharp enough to chop the shark in half. Placoderms like this were once the largest, fiercest carnivores of all.

Name	*Dunkleosteus*
Pronunciation	dun-klee-os-TAY-us
Meaning	"Dunkle's bony one"
Class	Placodermi
Order	Arthrodira
Length	Up to 30 ft (9 m)
Food	Other fishes
Location	Oceans
Era	Paleozoic
Period	Devonian (*c.*365 mya)

545		248	65	0
Proterozoic	Paleozoic		Mesozoic	Cenozoic

STETHACANTHUS

Sharks are streamlined, torpedo-shaped hunters of the seas, but a long, narrow tower rather like a submarine's conning tower sprouted from the back of *Stethacanthus*'s head. From this tower's flat top sprouted a brush of pointed scales that looked like sharp little teeth.

Scientists believe that only the males possessed this fancy headgear. Mating females might have connected to this spine brush much as females grasped the far narrower fin spines of some

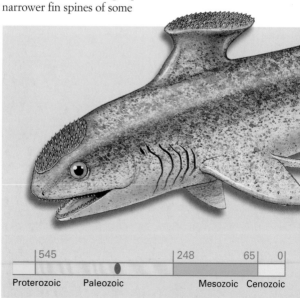

545		248	65	0
Proterozoic	Paleozoic		Mesozoic	Cenozoic

other stethacanthid sharks. But there is another possibility. The spine brush matched a clump of pointed tooth-like scales on the head below. Seen head-on, both clumps perhaps resembled a pair of gaping jaws; enough to scare off powerful enemies.

Like other sharks, *Stethacanthus* had a skeleton made of lightweight gristle, not bone. And like other sharks it had to keep swimming. If it stopped, it sank and suffocated.

Name	*Stethacanthus*
Pronunciation	steth-a-KAN-thus
Meaning	"Spiny chest"
Class	Chondrichthyes
Order	Symmoriida
Family	Stethacanthidae
Length	Under 3 ft 3 in (1 m)
Food	Small fishes
Location	Oceans
Era	Paleozoic
Period	Devonian-Carboniferous (370–350 mya)

CLIMATIUS

Little *Climatius* had a blunt head, narrow, streamlined body, and upturned tail. At first glance it looked like some living fishes, but bristled with two spiky fins on its back and 3 spiky fins and 10 sharp spines beneath.

Such so-called "spiny sharks" were among the first fishes with hinged jaws. Like true sharks they kept growing new teeth as their old ones fell out. Again like sharks they had a springy backbone of gristle. But bony

Name *Climatius*
Pronunciation KLIME-AT-ee-us
Meaning "Inclined" [fish]
Class Acanthodii
Order Climatiiformes
Family Climatiidae
Length 3 in (7.5 cm)
Food Tiny fishes etc
Location Canada, UK
Era Paleozoic
Period Silurian–Devonian
(c.410–400 mya)

scales protected their bodies, especially the head and shoulders. Perhaps these marine and freshwater fishes were close to the ancestors of fishes with bony skeletons.

Climatius perhaps zoomed over riverbeds, its big eyes helping it to spot the creatures it hunted for food. With a flick of its tail, *Climatius* caught and snapped up little fishes and crustaceans. Spines and armor helped to prevent it ending up inside big hungry fishes itself.

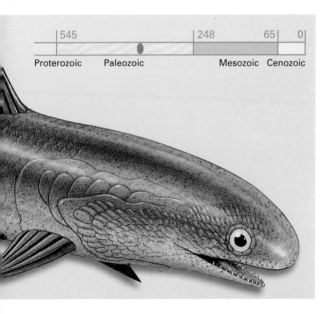

545		248	65	0
Proterozoic	Paleozoic		Mesozoic	Cenozoic

LEEDSICHTHYS

This might have been the biggest fish ever. The largest species perhaps reached 100 feet (30 m). That is more than half as long again as the whale shark, today's record holder weighing up to 44 tons (40 tonnes). Unlike sharks, *Leedsichthys* had a bony not a gristly skeleton.

Leedsichthys's body tapered at both ends, with a deep, V-shaped tail at one end, and a great head reinforced by bony plates at the other. The mouth was huge. Near the gill

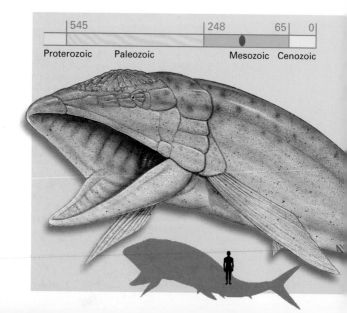

545		248	65	0
Proterozoic	Paleozoic		Mesozoic	Cenozoic

covers, a pair of long, scythe-shaped pectoral fins fanned the water to brake or change direction.

Like whale sharks and basking sharks, *Leedsichthys* would have been a gentle giant: cruising slowly at the surface of the sea, mouth agape to suck in clouds of tiny organisms. Size was its main defense, but a sea crocodilian's tooth stuck in one individual's skull shows that big marine predators dared to attack it.

Name	*Leedsichthys*
Pronunciation	leedz-IK-this
Meaning	"Leeds' fish"
Class	Osteichthyes
Order	Pachycormiformes
Family	Pachycormidae
Length	49–98 ft (15–30 m)
Food	Tiny sea creatures
Location	Oceans worldwide
Era	Mesozoic
Period	Jurassic (*c.*160 mya)

PANDERICHTHYS

Panderichthys was a fish with four fins and a tail, yet similar creatures seem to have given rise to all backboned land animals, humans included.

This fierce freshwater predator had a head shaped rather like a tiny alligator's. It was long and broad with eyes on top and sharp-toothed jaws. The long, low body ended in a narrow, tapering tail, and all four fins were worked by fleshy, muscular lobes a bit like tiny, stumpy limbs.

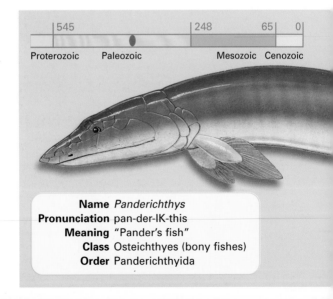

545		248	65	0
Proterozoic	Paleozoic		Mesozoic	Cenozoic

Name *Panderichthys*
Pronunciation pan-der-IK-this
Meaning "Pander's fish"
Class Osteichthyes (bony fishes)
Order Panderichthyida

The front pair of lobes was reinforced by tiny bones that matched those in a dog's forelimbs or your arms. The rear pair of lobes had bones to match those in a dog's hind limbs or your legs. Unlike most fishes, it had no fin on its back or under its body.

Scientists think that *Panderichthys* hunted tiny animals in warm, shallow water. Unlike most fishes, it could probably breathe air at the surface. Perhaps its stubby limbs even hauled it ashore, making it one of the first backboned animals to crawl about on land.

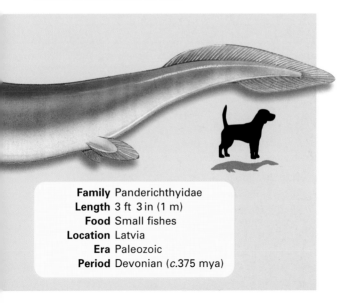

Family	Panderichthyidae
Length	3 ft 3 in (1 m)
Food	Small fishes
Location	Latvia
Era	Paleozoic
Period	Devonian (*c.*375 mya)

7. Amphibians and Early Tetrapods

ABOUT AMPHIBIANS

About 365 million years ago appeared the Tetrapoda (**1**), or four-limbed backboned animals. Tetrapods evolved from fishes with four fleshy lobes working fins to lever themselves along through shallow water.

Early tetrapods included the Ichthyostegalia (**2**), with toes and fingers, but also gills and other fishy features.

Such creatures gave rise to several evolutionary lines, all often known as amphibians, which means "both kinds of life." Many amphibians lived both on land and in the water. Such sprawling carnivores breathed air with lungs or through their skin but laid their shell-less eggs in water to stop them drying up. The class Amphibia (**3**) arguably included the extinct Temnospondyli (**4**) and Nectridea (**5**), as well as Lissamphibia: frogs and salamanders (**6**).

A second evolutionary line of tetrapods produced the Anthracosauria (**7**) or "coal lizards." Among these were animals whose sturdy limbs made them better built for life on land than the amphibians. Such creatures were to give rise to the reptiles.

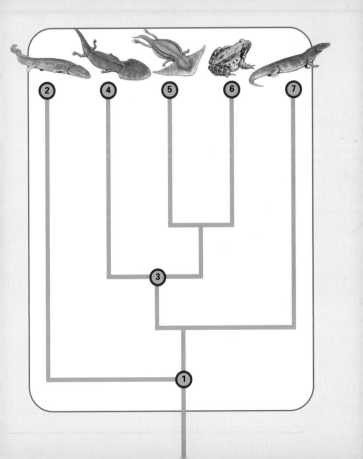

ACANTHOSTEGA

Acanthostega was a pioneering tetrapod (four-footed backboned animal.) With four limbs but fishlike gills it was an evolutionary missing link between bony fishes such as *Panderichthys* and their living descendants, the amphibians, reptiles, birds, and mammals.

At first glance *Acanthostega* resembled a large, long-bodied salamander, with a low, broad head, and a deep, flattened tail. There were big differences, though. For instance, fishy

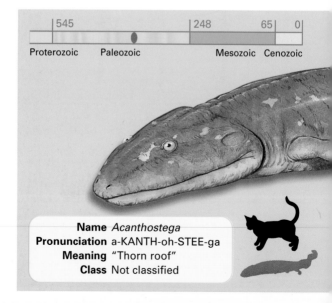

545		248	65	0
Proterozoic	Paleozoic		Mesozoic	Cenozoic

Name *Acanthostega*
Pronunciation a-KANTH-oh-STEE-ga
Meaning "Thorn roof"
Class Not classified

fin rays reinforced its tail, and each of its weak, short limbs ended in eight "fingers" or eight "toes." Later tetrapods had five digits on each limb at most.

Scientists believe that *Acanthostega* ambushed small fishes and crustaceans in weedy, shallow pools. The short limbs served as props to keep it off the bottom, and as poles to punt itself along. This early tetrapod was not a true amphibian and most probably it never left water.

Order	Ichthyostegalia
Family	Acanthostegidae
Length	2 ft (60 cm)
Food	Small fishes, etc.
Location	Greenland
Era	Paleozoic
Period	Devonian (*c.*362 mya)

KOOLASUCHUS

This gigantic relative of today's small newts and salamanders grew as long as a large car, and probably weighed up to half a ton.

Koolasuchus sprawled sluggishly on land. Its limbs were too short and weak to prop up its heavy body. In lakes and rivers, though, it swam quite fast by pressing its legs against its sides and waggling its long, deep, narrow tail. Submerged, the huge amphibian ambushed passing creatures. As it sensed vibrations in the water its massive

Name *Koolasuchus*
Pronunciation KOOL-a-SOOK-us
Meaning "Kool's crocodile"
Class Amphibia

545		248	65	0
Proterozoic	Paleozoic		Mesozoic	Cenozoic

jaws yawned open then snapped shut upon a lungfish or a turtle. Even small dinosaurs that came to drink were not safe from this ferocious, flabby monster.

Koolasuchus was a living fossil in its time, an Australian amphibian that played the part of crocodiles in other continents. There, competition from these big strong-bodied reptiles had killed off its relatives 100 million years before.

Order	Temnospondyli
Family	Plagiosauridae
Length	16 ft 6 in (5 m)
Food	Fishes, turtles, etc.
Location	Australia
Era	Mesozoic
Period	Cretaceous (*c.*112–104 mya)

DIPLOCAULUS

Diplocaulus was one of the oddest-looking of all prehistoric animals. Bones at the back of its flat skull flared out to each side as it grew, producing a head shaped like a cocked hat or a boomerang. For such a large head, its flat body and tail seem rather short, and its weak limbs were unsuited for walking on land.

This newtlike amphibian lived entirely in water. Most probably it lurked at the bottom of rivers and pools,

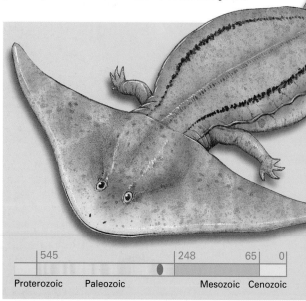

545		248	65	0
Proterozoic	Paleozoic		Mesozoic	Cenozoic

catching crustaceans and fishes in its small mouth. Perhaps its wide head worked like a submarine's diving planes: angling it up or down helped its owner to rise or dive. Or perhaps male rivals sideswiped one another with their heads, or their width made hungry predators suppose that *Diplocaulus* was too much of a mouthful to swallow.

Diplocaulus belonged to the lepospondyls, a mixed group perhaps including the ancestors of lissamphibians, the modern amphibians.

Name	*Diplocaulus*
Pronunciation	DIP-loe-KAW-lus
Meaning	"Double caul"
Class	Amphibia
Order	Nectridea
Family	Keraterpetontidae
Length	3 ft 3 in (1 m)
Food	Small animals
Location	North America (Texas)
Era	Paleozoic
Period	Permian (*c.*275–260 mya)

SEYMOURIA

Short, stout *Seymouria* was better built for life on land than early amphibians. A well developed hip and shoulder girdle, sturdy limb bones, and fairly long limbs helped it to move quite fast. Anything slower and smaller than itself, even another *Seymouria,* could end between its sharp little cone-shaped teeth, including some in the roof of its mouth. Other clues that it lived out of water include a reptilian neck joint, and a skull with a hint of an eardrum and

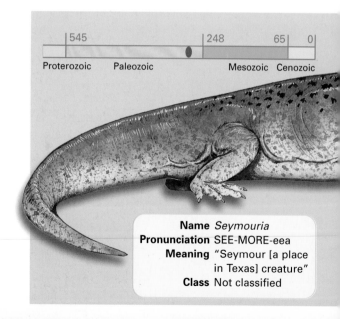

545		248	65	0
Proterozoic	Paleozoic		Mesozoic	Cenozoic

Name *Seymouria*
Pronunciation SEE-MORE-eea
Meaning "Seymour [a place in Texas] creature"
Class Not classified

middle-ear bone for detecting airborne sounds higher than any that fishes hear under water.

Scientists once supposed *Seymouria* had been a primitive reptile. Then someone discovered such creatures' fossil young with lateral-line canals in their skulls. Similar structures help fishes to sense vibrations in water, so *Seymouria* had been amphibious, returning to water to breed. Even so, some lump it with the anthracosaurs: tetrapods that gave rise to reptiles and mammals.

Order	Anthracosauria
Family	Seymouriidae
Length	2 ft (60 cm)
Food	Meat
Location	North America, Europe
Era	Paleozoic
Period	Permian (280–270 mya)

8. Reptiles

ABOUT REPTILES

Living reptiles are cold-blooded, backboned animals with dry, scaly skin. Like birds and mammals, they are amniotes: tetrapods that can breed on land by producing eggs containing moisture and nourishment and protected from drying up. Prehistoric tetrapods gave rise to reptiles (the Reptilia) (**1**) by 300 million years ago.

From small, lizard-like insect-eaters came the creatures in this chapter. The Mesosauria (**2**) and Captorhinida (**3**) were early anapsids, with no skull holes behind each eye. Most later reptiles were diapsids, with two holes. Diapsids designed for

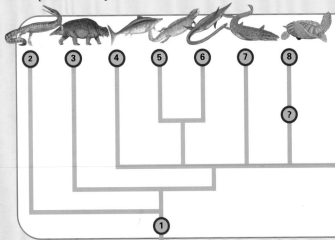

life at sea included the Ichthyopterygia (ichthyosaurs) (**4**), Placodontia (placodonts) (**5**), and Plesiosauria (plesiosaurs) (**6**). The Squamata (snakes and lizards) (**7**) and Chelonia (turtles) (**8**) include living species. The Archosauromorpha ("ruling reptile forms") (**9**) included the Rhynchosauria (rhynchosaurs) (**10**) and Protorosauria (protorosaurs) (**11**) and two important groups: Crurotarsi ("cross ankles") (**12**) and Ornithodira ("bird necks"). The Crurotarsi included the Crocodylia (crocodilians) (**13**), Rauisuchia (rauisuchians) (**14**), and Aetosauria (aetosaurs) (**15**). Among the Ornithodira (**16**) were the Pterosauria (pterosaurs) (**17**) and Dinosauria (dinosaurs) (**18**). Dinosaurs formed two main groups: Ornithischia (ornithischians) (**19**) and Saurischia (saurischians) (**20**).

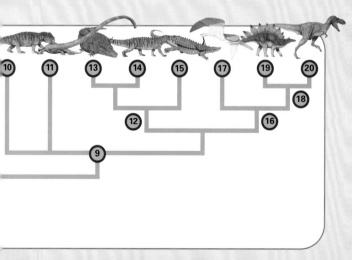

MESOSAURUS

Mesosaurus resembled a long-bodied lizard shaped for swimming. Its hips and shoulders were too weak for sturdy walking. Instead, it swam by waggling its tail, very probably equipped with a fin, and braked with broad, webbed feet that worked as paddles.

The narrow head was rather like a crocodile's, with eyes set far back, and elongated jaws. Unlike crocodile jaws, though, *Mesosaurus*'s bristled with slender teeth like knitting needles. When its mouth closed, the top and bottom teeth

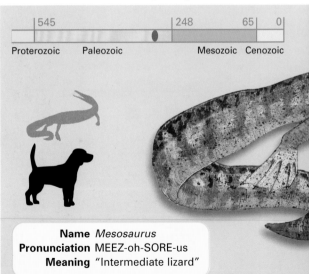

	545			248	65	0
	Proterozoic	Paleozoic			Mesozoic	Cenozoic

Name *Mesosaurus*
Pronunciation MEEZ-oh-SORE-us
Meaning "Intermediate lizard"

meshed together, trapping little fishes or crustaceans and letting water in the mouth strain away.

Mesosaurus is famous for two reasons. This small inshore swimmer was one of the first reptiles to return to the water, from which all reptiles' ancestors had come. Secondly, its fossils turn up in Africa and South America, a proof that both had once been joined.

Class	Reptilia
Order	Mesosauria
Family	Mesosauridae
Length	3 ft 3 in (1 m)
Food	Crustaceans and fishes
Location	Brazil and Africa
Era	Paleozoic
Period	Permian (*c.*280 mya)

SCUTOSAURUS

Think of a heavy, deep-bodied beast bigger than a pygmy hippopotamus and you get some idea of *Scutosaurus.* Details of its small, spiny skull show that this squat, ugly animal belonged to the primitive reptiles called *anapsids*.

Scutosaurus was far larger than its little, lizard-like ancestors, and, instead of sprawling, stood on four strong limbs that held its bulky body well up off the ground. Anapsids built to this plan are called *pareiasaurs.*

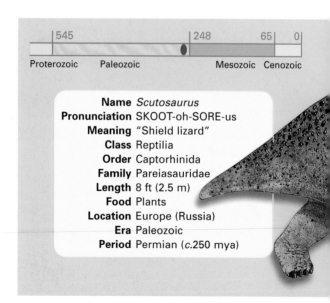

	545		248	65	0
	Proterozoic	Paleozoic		Mesozoic	Cenozoic

Name	*Scutosaurus*
Pronunciation	SKOOT-oh-SORE-us
Meaning	"Shield lizard"
Class	Reptilia
Order	Captorhinida
Family	Pareiasauridae
Length	8 ft (2.5 m)
Food	Plants
Location	Europe (Russia)
Era	Paleozoic
Period	Permian (*c.*250 mya)

Teeth like an iguana lizard's and a barrel-shaped body roomy enough to hold a large gut make scientists think that *Scutosaurus* ate bulky vegetation. Some suspect it waded into pools and munched floating water plants.

Big meat-eaters might have hesitated to attack this stocky creature, with bony knobs set in its thick, leathery skin. Wide-bodied, armored reptiles like this just might have given rise to the tortoises and turtles.

OPHTHALMOSAURUS

Of those many reptiles that returned to water, the finest swimmers were the streamlined ichthyosaurs ("fish lizards"), especially dolphin-shaped *Ophthalmosaurus.*

Behind its narrow, pointed snout the body swelled, then tapered to a tall tail like a fish's. By waggling its tail, the ichthyosaur powered through the sea as fast as road-race cyclists ride the Tour de France. Steering and braking with

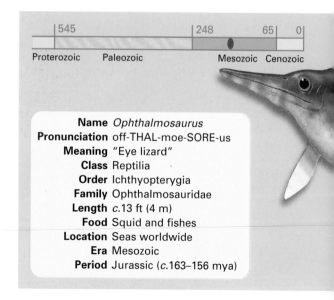

545		248	65	0
Proterozoic	Paleozoic		Mesozoic	Cenozoic

Name	*Ophthalmosaurus*
Pronunciation	off-THAL-moe-SORE-us
Meaning	"Eye lizard"
Class	Reptilia
Order	Ichthyopterygia
Family	Ophthalmosauridae
Length	*c.*13 ft (4 m)
Food	Squid and fishes
Location	Seas worldwide
Era	Mesozoic
Period	Jurassic (*c.*163–156 mya)

large front flippers, it snapped up squid and fishes. Scientists believe it dived deep after prey. With eyes as big as bowling balls (the largest eyes of any backboned animal) it could have spotted faint lights given off by creatures in the soot-black gloom about 2,000 feet (600 m) below the surface. A round trip would have taken only 20 minutes. Proof that *Ophthalmosaurus* dived deep comes from damage suffered by its bones, inflicted by gas bubbles that expanded in its body as it rose.

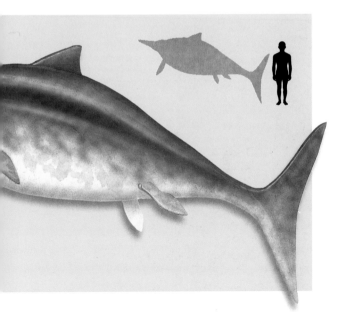

PLACODUS

Placodus belonged to the placodonts: reptiles with broad bodies, and powerful beaks or teeth for cracking open shellfish. Placodonts ate bivalves and brachiopods living on submerged rocks near a sea shore.

Placodus was not a strong swimmer. Its tail was probably too shallow to waggle like a newt's. The "toes" and "fingers" were too short to make large paddles, but webbed skin

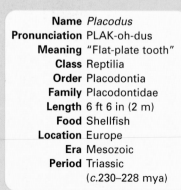

Name	*Placodus*
Pronunciation	PLAK-oh-dus
Meaning	"Flat-plate tooth"
Class	Reptilia
Order	Placodontia
Family	Placodontidae
Length	6 ft 6 in (2 m)
Food	Shellfish
Location	Europe
Era	Mesozoic
Period	Triassic (*c.*230–228 mya)

between their digits might have helped this reptile to swim slowly in its search for underwater food.

The creature had no need for speed: no large enemies to dodge or agile prey to chase. Using spoon-shaped "buck" front teeth, it simply prized molluscs from their rocks. Then it set to work with powerful jaws. Flat cheek teeth and huge flat tooth plates like millstones in the mouth roof crushed its victims' shells. *Placodus* swallowed the meat and spat out the shards.

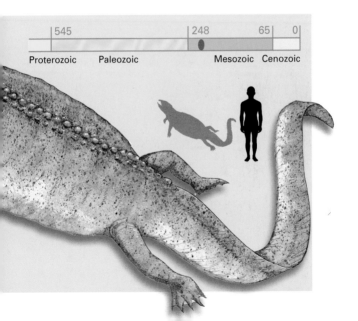

545 248 65 0

Proterozoic Paleozoic Mesozoic Cenozoic

ELASMOSAURUS

Elasmosaurus was as long as a grey whale, but with its slim neck and broad body it looked like most people's idea of the Loch Ness monster.

This big swimming reptile belonged to the plesiosaurs ("near lizards"). It had a small head, an incredibly long, snaky neck; a barrel-shaped body; broad ribs; extra ribs protecting its belly; four long, flat flippers; and a short tail.

Name	*Elasmosaurus*
Pronunciation	i-laz-moh-SORE-us
Meaning	"Metal-plated lizard"
Class	Reptilia
Order	Plesiosauria
Family	Elasmosauridae
Location	North America (Kansas)
Length	46 ft (14 m)
Food	Fish
Location	North America
Era	Mesozoic
Period	Late Cretaceous (*c.*80 mya)

More than 70 bones strengthened the neck, which took up more than half the creature's entire length.

Elasmosaurus hunted fish in a shallow sea that once covered much of North America. It swam by beating its flippers up and down, and darted its head from side to side, seizing slippery prey with its sharp slender teeth. Plesiosaurs might have hauled themselves ashore to lay eggs on a beach, but some people doubt they could do this. Perhaps they gave birth to live young at sea.

545		248	65	0
Proterozoic	Paleozoic		Mesozoic	Cenozoic

LIOPLEURODON

Pliosaurs (short-necked plesiosaurs) included the biggest big-game hunters of Jurassic seas. Among the most gigantic of them all was *Liopleurodon*. Calculations hint at a predator more than twice as long as a killer whale, with a head the length of a small car.

Liopleurodon might have been the largest carnivorous animal of all time. Its weapons were sharp, pointed teeth twice as long as *Tyrannosaurus*'s, clustered in a formidable

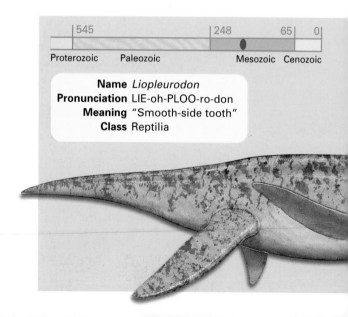

545		248	65	0
Proterozoic	Paleozoic		Mesozoic	Cenozoic

Name	*Liopleurodon*
Pronunciation	LIE-oh-PLOO-ro-don
Meaning	"Smooth-side tooth"
Class	Reptilia

rosette around the tip of its elongated jaws capable of wrenching large victims into bite-sized chunks.

Four broad limbs designed as paddles thrust this reptile's whale-sized body powerfully along. In dimly lit waters, a keen sense of smell helped *Liopleurodon* to home in on unsuspecting swimming reptiles smaller than itself. Evidence of *Liopleurodon*'s huge appetite includes the fossil remains of half-eaten ichthyosaurs, and plesiosaur limb bones with punch marks made by pliosaur teeth.

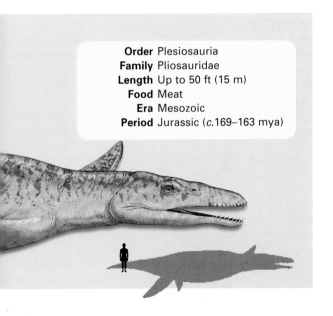

Order	Plesiosauria
Family	Pliosauridae
Length	Up to 50 ft (15 m)
Food	Meat
Era	Mesozoic
Period	Jurassic (*c*.169–163 mya)

ICAROSAURUS

Icarosaurus was like a lizard but with primitive features including teeth in its mouth roof, as well as its jaws. Its most striking features, though, were wings. Long before any bird flew, *Icarosaurus* and several similar creatures were gliding from tree to tree, much like today's so-called flying lizard of Southeast Asia.

Each wing consisted of incredibly extended ribs joined by skin webbing. *Icarosaurus* would climb trees with its wings

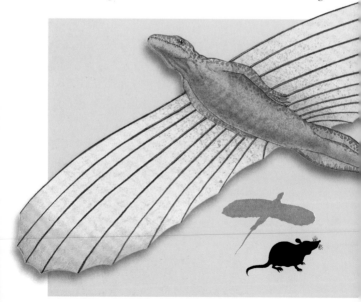

folded back and their webs loose and floppy. When it leapt off a tree, the ribs swung forward, stretching the webs and making them taut.

Icarosaurus could probably zoom 200 feet (60 m) across a forest glade and land on the trunk of another tree only 6 feet 6 inches (2 m) lower than its takeoff point. By gliding to forage for tree-living insects it saved energy. It also avoided hungry predators that only hunted on the ground.

Name	*Icarosaurus*
Pronunciation	IK-a-roe-SORE-us
Meaning	"Icarus lizard"
Class	Reptilia
Order	Not specified
Family	Kuehneosauridae

545		248	65	0
Proterozoic	Paleozoic		Mesozoic	Cenozoic

Length	6 in (15 cm)
Food	Insects
Location	North America
Era	Mesozoic
Period	Triassic
	(*c.*220–210 mya)

TYLOSAURUS

Spectacularly huge lizards swarmed in Late Cretaceous seas. As long as a badminton court, *Tylosaurus* was a giant among these mosasaurs, related to monitor lizards. Unlike them it was born and lived entirely in water. A deep tail snakily waving from side to side drove this monster through the sea. The forelimbs formed large paddles; hind limbs were much smaller and weaker. This hunter's weapons

	545		248	65	0
	Proterozoic	Paleozoic		Mesozoic	Cenozoic

were a sharp, bony snout and toothy jaws in a man-length head. Long, pointed teeth rimmed its jaws and extra teeth jutted from the mouth roof.

Tylosaurus's snout could have knocked out sizable animals, and once its teeth clamped on a victim the slipperiest could not escape. Dislocating its jaws like a snake, it swallowed large creatures whole. One individual's last meal was a diving bird, a shark, a bony fish, and a mosasaur half as long as itself.

Name	*Tylosaurus*
Pronunciation	TIE-loe-SORE-us
Meaning	"knob lizard"

Class	Reptilia
Order	Squamata
Family	Mosasauridae
Length	Up to 46 ft (14 m)
Food	Meat
Location	North America, New Zealand
Era	Mesozoic
Period	Cretaceous (*c.*85–80 mya)

PACHYRHACHIS

Pachyrhachis looked like a snake but had two little legs designed like a lizard's. It was about the length of a man's leg, with a small, narrow, skull, no forelimbs, and almost uselessly tiny hind limbs.

Traces of hind limb bones in many snakes' skeletons had made scientists suspect that these reptiles evolved from burrowing lizards whose limbs dwindled or vanished because they got in the

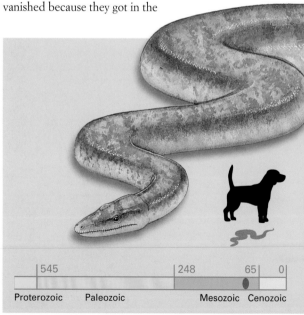

545		248	65	0
Proterozoic	Paleozoic		Mesozoic	Cenozoic

way underground. In the 1990s, a new look at *Pachyrhachis* suggested this idea might be wrong. Most of its anatomical features were those of a snake, yet *Pachyrhachis* had the ankle joints of a mosasaur lizard. Like its mosasauroid ancestors, this most primitive snake had caught fishes and swum in a sea.

Pachyrhachis hints that snakes came from lizards that lost the need for limbs because they swam eel-fashion, limbs pressed to their bodies to reduce water resistance.

Name	Pachyrhachis
Pronunciation	PAK-ee-RAKE-is
Meaning	"Thick backbone"
Class	Reptilia
Order	Squamata
Family	Pachyophiidae
Length	3 ft 3 in (1 m)
Food	Fishes
Location	Israel
Era	Mesozoic
Period	Cretaceous (*c.*97 mya)

ARCHELON

As long as a large car and even longer between its outstretched front flippers, this Late Cretaceous sea turtle outstripped all others. Flapping its flippers up and down like a penguin's wings, it "flew" through the water, seizing jellyfish in its toothless hooked beak.

Most turtles have a thick shell formed from a bony carapace guarding the back and a plastron guarding the belly. A threatened

Name	*Archelon*
Pronunciation	ar-KEE-lon
Meaning	"King turtle"
Class	Reptilia
Order	Chelonia
Family	Protostegidae
Length	Up to 15 ft (4.5 m)
Food	Jellyfish
Location	North America
Era	Mesozoic
Period	Cretaceous (*c.*74 mya)

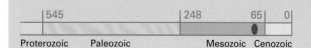

545		248	65	0
Proterozoic	Paleozoic		Mesozoic	Cenozoic

tortoise can pull head, limbs and tail inside its massive shell to protect them. To save weight, *Archelon*'s shell was reduced to small plates on a framework of struts formed by the ribs. Thick, rubbery skin like a leatherback turtle's probably covered the lot.

Archelon evolved from freshwater turtles derived from land tortoises. All had solidly roofed skulls like the long-extinct pareiasaurs, but other clues hint that turtles shared the same ancestor as lizards and crocodiles.

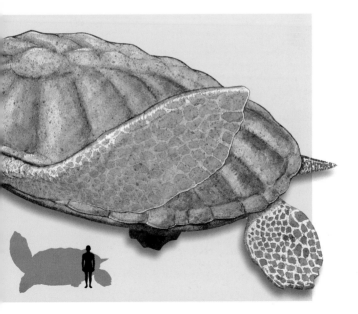

SCAPHONYX

Scaphonyx belonged to the squat, piglike rhynchosaurs or "snout lizards." Remote relatives of the dinosaurs' ancestors, these were once plentiful nearly worldwide.

Scaphonyx had short legs, a heavy body, and a broad, deep, triangular head with two strange pairs of bony tusks working like tongs. The upper jaw's downcurved tusks closed between the lower jaw's upcurved tusks. Farther back, small peg-shaped teeth in the knifelike lower

Name	*Scaphonyx*
Pronunciation	SKAF-ON-iks
Meaning	"Boat-shaped claw"
Class	Reptilia
Order	Rhynchosauria
Family	Rhynchosauridae
Length	6 ft (1.8 m)

jaw fitted into grooves in the upper jaw's two broad toothplates, each studded with rows of small teeth.

The massive jaw muscles delivered a crushing bite. Some scientists have suggested this strange reptile crunched up freshwater clams. Most think it ate tough vegetation. It could have dug up tubers and roots with its tusks or strong hind feet, chopped them up with its teeth, and digested them in its barrel-shaped body.

Food	Plants
Location	South America
Era	Mesozoic
Period	Triassic
	(*c.*228–225 mya)

545		248	65	0
Proterozoic	Paleozoic		Mesozoic	Cenozoic

TANYSTROPHEUS

Tanystropheus must be a strong contender for the prize of weirdest looking reptile of all time. Its body, legs, and tail looked somewhat like a lizard's, yet tail and body put together were shorter than its narrow, rodlike neck. This appeared as impossibly long as the victim's neck in a film cartoon where people pulling opposite ways stretch a neck like elastic. Yet only 9 to 12 extremely elongated bones supported the neck and tiny head.

Name	*Tanystropheus*
Pronunciation	TAN-i-STROF-ee-us
Meaning	"Stretched vertebrae"
Class	Reptilia
Order	Protorosauria
Family	Tanystropheidae
Length	10 ft (3 m)

The bizarre creature inhabited the shores of an ancient sea that covered much of what is now Europe. Its young had relatively short necks and three-pointed teeth. Very probably they lived on land and ate insects. The adults' weak legs and front-heavy design meant these might have needed water to support their weight. Perhaps they swam and paddled in the shallows, or angled from the water's edge: swinging necks like living fishing rods and seizing fish between their teeth, now shaped as simple pegs.

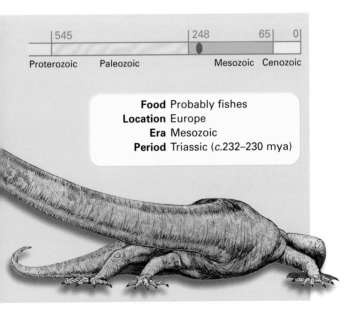

545		248	65	0
Proterozoic	Paleozoic		Mesozoic	Cenozoic

Food Probably fishes
Location Europe
Era Mesozoic
Period Triassic (c.232–230 mya)

DESMATOSUCHUS

Desmatosuchus resembled a cross between a crocodile and an armadillo. It belonged to the aetosaurs, once lumped with various reptiles under the name thecodonts ("socket-toothed creatures"). All were archosaurs ("ruling reptiles") a group including the crocodiles and dinosaurs.

This animal had a small, piglike head, and long, heavy body and tail, and it walked on short, erect legs. Its narrow

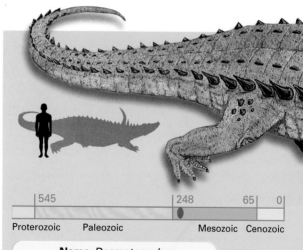

545		248	65	0
Proterozoic	Paleozoic		Mesozoic	Cenozoic

Name *Desmatosuchus*
Pronunciation des-mat-oh-SOOK-us
Meaning "Crocodile link"

snout jutted out beyond a lower jaw curved like a lady's slipper. Small teeth rimmed its jaws except at the toothless front of the mouth. Bands of thick bony plates arranged crosswise protected the bulky body's back, flanks, and belly, and covered the tail. Spines more than half as long as a man's arm guarded the shoulders.

Desmatosuchus could have shoveled up edible roots with its snout, and munched horsetails and ferns. Big carnivorous archosaurs were its worst enemies.

Class	Reptilia
Order	Aetosauria
Family	Stagonolepididae
Length	16 ft (5 m)
Food	Plants
Location	North America
Era	Mesozoic
Period	Triassic (*c.*230–225 mya)

POSTOSUCHUS

Small, early dinosaurs in what are now Arizona and Texas gave a wide berth to *Postosuchus*. This was a rauisuchian, a type of large hunting archosaur reptile related to crocodiles. It was the top predator of its day.

Postosuchus weighed as much as a buffalo and grew as long as a family car. Rows of bony plates formed the armor protecting its back, and the large, deep head bore powerful jaws with sharp, saw-edged, "steak knife" teeth. The

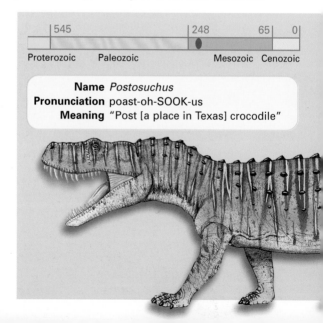

545		248	65	0
Proterozoic	Paleozoic		Mesozoic	Cenozoic

Name *Postosuchus*
Pronunciation poast-oh-SOOK-us
Meaning "Post [a place in Texas] crocodile"

scientist who named it thought it had walked on its long hindlimbs balanced by its muscular tail, but most experts believe it walked on four limbs, held upright.

Postosuchus could attack aetosaurs or other large plant-eating reptiles. If it was too slow to catch them by chasing it might have hidden among trees, then suddenly lunged, using the sharp claws of its "hands" to hook onto its prey, while sinking its teeth in their flesh.

Class	Reptilia
Order	Rauisuchia
Family	Rauisuchidae
Length	15 ft (4.5 m)
Food	Meat
Location	North America
Era	Mesozoic
Period	Triassic (*c*.225 mya)

DEINOSUCHUS

The age of giant dinosaurs was also an age of giant crocodilians, with *Deinosuchus* perhaps the largest of all.

This broad-snouted, alligator-like beast could have swallowed a man in one gulp. It weighed as much as an elephant and from nose to tail could have spanned the width of a tennis court. The secret of its great size seems to be that *Deinosuchus* grew fast for most of its life, not, like

modern alligators and crocodiles, only while young. It outlived these, too, exceeding 50 years.

Deinosuchus lurked in North American swamps between what are now Montana and Texas. Lying like a half-submerged tree trunk near the water's edge, it suddenly clamped its vast jaws on any unwary duck-billed dinosaur bending to drink. Scientists suspect that this fearsome beast killed far more large plant-eating dinosaurs than *Tyrannosaurus* or its relatives did.

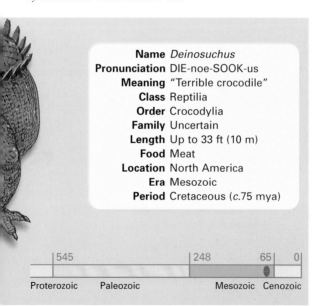

Name	*Deinosuchus*
Pronunciation	DIE-noe-SOOK-us
Meaning	"Terrible crocodile"
Class	Reptilia
Order	Crocodylia
Family	Uncertain
Length	Up to 33 ft (10 m)
Food	Meat
Location	North America
Era	Mesozoic
Period	Cretaceous (*c.*75 mya)

545		248	65	0
Proterozoic	Paleozoic		Mesozoic	Cenozoic

PTERODAUSTRO

Pterodaustro was the strangest looking of all those prehistoric fliers, the pterosaurs: reptiles with skin wings whose leading edges mostly consisted of the fourth fingers' bones stretched out to extraordinary lengths.

This pterosaur's weirdest feature was its head's enormously long, narrow, upcurved beak crammed with teeth and bristles. The upper teeth were short and tiny, but a thousand, long, close-packed, springy bristles sprouted

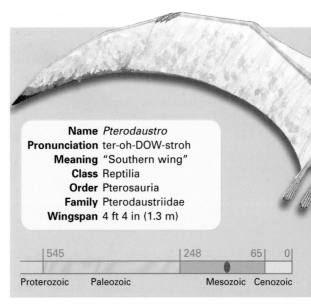

Name	*Pterodaustro*
Pronunciation	ter-oh-DOW-stroh
Meaning	"Southern wing"
Class	Reptilia
Order	Pterosauria
Family	Pterodaustriidae
Wingspan	4 ft 4 in (1.3 m)

545		248	65	0
Proterozoic	Paleozoic		Mesozoic	Cenozoic

from its lower jaw. Like teeth on two combs, meeting at the beak tip, these formed a bristle basket.

Skimming over shallow lagoons, *Pterodaustro* dipped its beak below the surface, sieved tiny organisms from the water, and licked off any sticking to the inside of its bristly trap. Wading flamingos trawl their beaks through water much like this today. Perhaps the pterosaur's top teeth chopped up food too large to swallow.

Food	Tiny organisms
Location	South America
Era	Mesozoic
Period	Cretaceous (*c.*140 mya)

QUETZALCOATLUS

Picture a gigantic stork with a microlight aircraft's wingspan and you get an idea of this outsize pterosaur's appearance. *Quetzalcoatlus* was one of the largest-ever creatures capable of flight.

The animal had a narrow, tapering beak; elongated neck; immensely long skin wings with short, clawed fingers at the leading edge; and scaly legs with clawed toes. Like other advanced pterosaurs it lacked teeth and a bony tail, and the

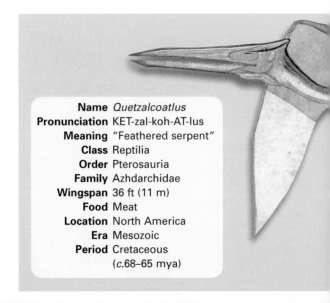

Name *Quetzalcoatlus*
Pronunciation KET-zal-koh-AT-lus
Meaning "Feathered serpent"
Class Reptilia
Order Pterosauria
Family Azhdarchidae
Wingspan 36 ft (11 m)
Food Meat
Location North America
Era Mesozoic
Period Cretaceous
(*c.*68–65 mya)

bones supporting its neck and wings were hollow, thin-walled, lightweight tubes. As big as a man, Quetzalcoatlus probably weighed no more than a child.

This pterosaur lived in inland North America as the Age of Dinosaurs ended. Perhaps warm rising air helped it to take off and soar, occasionally flapping its vast wings. Vulture-like, perhaps it gobbled dead dinosaurs' flesh, or, storklike, stood in shallow water catching fishes.

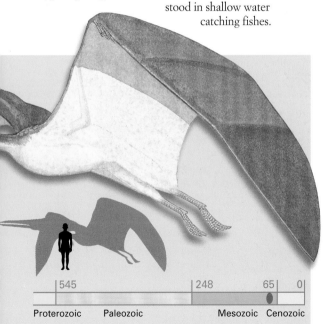

	545			248		65		0
Proterozoic		Paleozoic				Mesozoic	Cenozoic	

TYRANNOSAURUS

Tyrannosaurus was one of the last and largest theropods (meat-eating dinosaurs). Some individuals weighed more than 6.6 tons (6 tonnes). Maybe females grew larger than males.

The body was short and deep, the legs were immense. Yet the arms were tiny, with just two fingers on each hand. A strong, thick neck supported a colossal head about 3 feet (1m) long, with saw-edged fangs in jaws big enough to

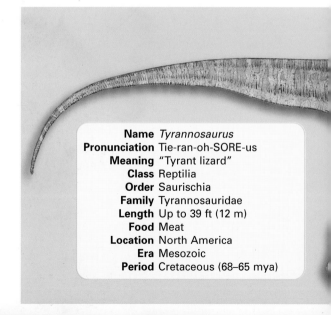

Name	*Tyrannosaurus*
Pronunciation	Tie-ran-oh-SORE-us
Meaning	"Tyrant lizard"
Class	Reptilia
Order	Saurischia
Family	Tyrannosauridae
Length	Up to 39 ft (12 m)
Food	Meat
Location	North America
Era	Mesozoic
Period	Cretaceous (68–65 mya)

swallow humans whole, had any been around. Yet the skull was lighter than you might expect, for many of its bones were only hollow struts.

Both forward-facing eyes could focus on one object. This might have helped *Tyrannosaurus* to judge if a horned dinosaur or hadrosaur was near enough to catch. It could not run fast enough to grab speedy prey. Some scientists think it ate only dinosaurs it found already dead.

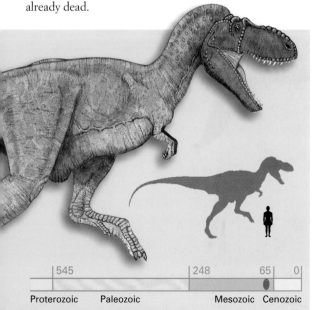

	545		248	65	0
Proterozoic		Paleozoic		Mesozoic	Cenozoic

CAUDIPTERYX

Twenty-five million years after dinosaurs seemingly gave rise to birds, long-legged "dinobirds" like this still lingered on in what is now China. Turkey-sized *Caudipteryx* had birdlike feathered wings and tail yet the skull, hipbones, big toes and other features of a theropod dinosaur.

Its unusual mixture of ingredients included a downy body covering; short arms with clawed fingers and long feathers; a fan of showy feathers sprouting from a brief bony tail;

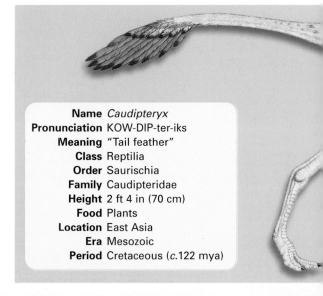

Name *Caudipteryx*
Pronunciation KOW-DIP-ter-iks
Meaning "Tail feather"
Class Reptilia
Order Saurischia
Family Caudipteridae
Height 2 ft 4 in (70 cm)
Food Plants
Location East Asia
Era Mesozoic
Period Cretaceous (*c.*122 mya)

and a beak that was entirely toothless except for spiky "buck" teeth jutting from its upper tip.

Caudipteryx ran fast but could not fly. Its feathers had the wrong design and its wings were too short. Instead, the downy body feathers kept it warm and males very probably fanned their tails and flapped their wings to show off to a rival or a mate. This dinobird ate plant foods, ground up by swallowed stones inside its gizzard.

	545		248	65	0
	Proterozoic	Paleozoic		Mesozoic	Cenozoic

BRACHIOSAURUS

Brachiosaurus was one of the largest land animals that ever lived. Some people think a well fed, full-grown specimen could have weighed as much as ten elephants.

This sauropod ("lizard-footed") dinosaur was built rather like a monstrous giraffe, with forelimbs longer than hind limbs and a deep body that sloped down from the shoulders to its relatively short and thickset tail.

545			248	65	0
Proterozoic	Paleozoic			Mesozoic	Cenozoic

To lighten the huge load held up by its limbs there were deeply scooped out spinal bones and a skull partly made of bony struts. As in all sauropods, nostrils opened high up on the head, which allowed *Brachiosaurus* to breathe while it ate.

Worn, chisel-shaped teeth suggest that this sauropod cropped tough leaves. *Brachiosaurus* might have nibbled leafy twigs high above ground level.

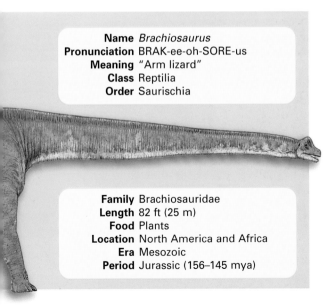

Name	*Brachiosaurus*
Pronunciation	BRAK-ee-oh-SORE-us
Meaning	"Arm lizard"
Class	Reptilia
Order	Saurischia

Family	Brachiosauridae
Length	82 ft (25 m)
Food	Plants
Location	North America and Africa
Era	Mesozoic
Period	Jurassic (156–145 mya)

STEGOSAURUS

Stegosaurus was the largest known plated dinosaur. It walked on all fours, with its deep, narrow body highest at the hips. The small, low-slung head was long and narrow, with a brain perhaps smaller than a dog's, tiny cheek teeth, and a toothless beak.

Stegosaurus might have been a choosy feeder, foraging for cycadeoids' and seed ferns' flowers and fruits. Perhaps it reared to nibble titbits above head level.

Name	*Stegosaurus*
Pronunciation	STEG-oh-SORE-us
Meaning	"Roof lizard"
Class	Reptilia
Order	Ornithischia
Family	Stegosauridae
Length	30 ft (9 m)
Food	Plants
Location	North America
Era	Mesozoic
Period	Jurassic (156–145 mya)

This slow-moving herbivore had armor for defense. Bony studs guarded its throat. Plates shielded its hips, and its long tail spikes could have swiped an enemy. Two staggered rows of tall bony plates rose from the neck, back, and upper tail. Too weak for armor, these might have scared rivals or attracted mates. Perhaps they also cooled or warmed *Stegosaurus* depending on whether it turned away from, or was broadside to the sun.

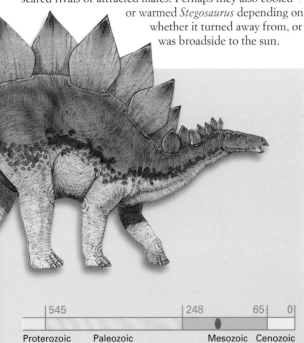

	545		248	65	0
	Proterozoic	Paleozoic		Mesozoic	Cenozoic

EUOPLOCEPHALUS

This large, four-legged, plant-eating ornithischian was one of the most heavily armored of all dinosaurs.

Euoplocephalus had a broad, heavy body, short neck, sturdy limbs, and a long tail held off the ground. Its reinforced skull was at least as wide as long, with a broad, toothless beak, and convoluted nasal passages.

Everything except its underside was armored. The head had bony horns, and slabs of horny scales like crazy paving

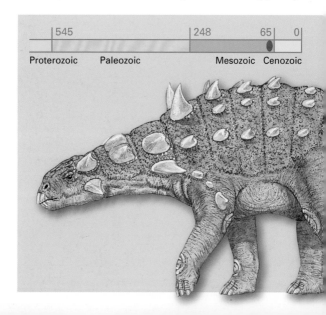

545		248	65	0
Proterozoic	Paleozoic		Mesozoic	Cenozoic

were stuck to its skull. There were even bony eyelids that flipped down like shutters to protect its eyes. Short, pointed, horn-sheathed, bony plates jutted from the shoulders and back. Bands of hollow-based plates set in the skin ran across the back and tail to protect them yet allow some flexibility. The swollen tail tip formed a heavy bony club. Swung from side to side, it might have knocked even an attacking *tyrannosaurid* off its feet.

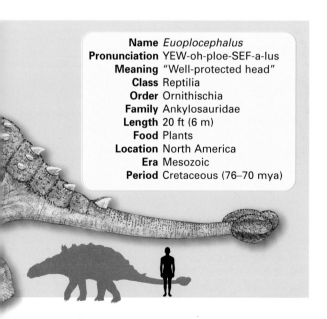

Name	*Euoplocephalus*
Pronunciation	YEW-oh-ploe-SEF-a-lus
Meaning	"Well-protected head"
Class	Reptilia
Order	Ornithischia
Family	Ankylosauridae
Length	20 ft (6 m)
Food	Plants
Location	North America
Era	Mesozoic
Period	Cretaceous (76–70 mya)

PARASAUROLOPHUS

Parasaurolophus was the most highly evolved of all
lambeosaurine hadrosaurs: duck-billed dinosaurs with a
hollow, bony head crest, larger in males than in females.

From *Parasaurolophus*'s head, a bony, curved tube 5 feet
(1.5 m) long projected back over the neck, perhaps
connected to it by a skin frill. The tube ran from the back
of the throat to the nostrils, doubling back on itself like the
tube of a trombone. Like a trombone, it amplified

sound. *Parasaurolophus*'s honking cry might have carried for miles. Like the showy head crest this call could have attracted mates or warned off rival males.

Apart from its built-in "trombone" this big, bulky plant-eater's head looked rather like a horse's, but with a blunt toothless beak, and batteries of self-sharpening cheek teeth for grinding up the leaves stored in cheek pouches. It walked on all fours but ran on the hind limbs.

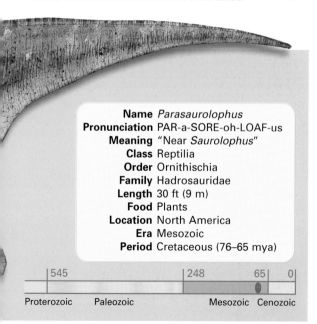

Name	*Parasaurolophus*
Pronunciation	PAR-a-SORE-oh-LOAF-us
Meaning	"Near *Saurolophus*"
Class	Reptilia
Order	Ornithischia
Family	Hadrosauridae
Length	30 ft (9 m)
Food	Plants
Location	North America
Era	Mesozoic
Period	Cretaceous (76–65 mya)

545		248	65	0
Proterozoic	Paleozoic		Mesozoic	Cenozoic

TRICERATOPS

Triceratops was one of the last and largest of the horned dinosaurs. Despite its short bony frill, other features of the skull persuade scientists that it belonged with the chasmosaurines, or long-frilled horned dinosaurs.

This great four-legged plant-eater weighed as much as an elephant and rather resembled a huge rhinoceros with an immense three-horned head. With its broad, bony frill at

545		248	65	0
Proterozoic	Paleozoic		Mesozoic	Cenozoic

the back, this was up to 7 feet 10 inches (2.4 m) long: one-third of this dinosaur's length. The nose horn was short but two very long brow horns jutted out over the eyes.

Old, healed injuries to *Triceratops* skulls might have been caused by these dinosaurs trying to fend off attacks by *Tyrannosaurus.* More likely they happened when rival males locked horns in battle. Usually, though, they probably just threatened each other by nodding their heads. The male with the largest head would have won.

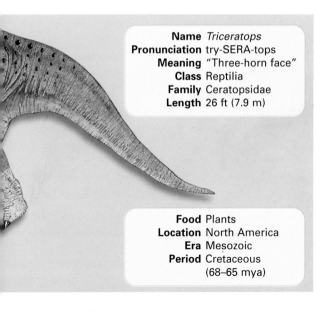

Name *Triceratops*
Pronunciation try-SERA-tops
Meaning "Three-horn face"
Class Reptilia
Family Ceratopsidae
Length 26 ft (7.9 m)

Food Plants
Location North America
Era Mesozoic
Period Cretaceous
(68–65 mya)

9. Birds

ABOUT BIRDS

Birds are warm-blooded, feathered, backboned animals with lightweight, hollow, air-filled bones. Most birds have forelimbs shaped as wings evolved for flight. Early birds had teeth, clawed fingers, and a long bony tail core. Apart from their reversed "big" toes they looked so like small, feathered theropods that most scientists think birds evolved from these predatory saurischian dinosaurs. Thus, although birds form a class of animals, Aves (**1**), this is arguably a subgroup of the class Reptilia.

The first known birds called Archaeopterygiformes (**2**) appeared about 150 million years ago. Later birds lost teeth and bony tail cores. Meanwhile, several groups of birds evolved along different lines. One might have been cold-blooded in the way that snakes and lizards are.

Most birds profiled in this chapter are prehistoric examples of five surviving orders in the only one surviving group of birds: Neornithes ("new birds") (**3**). Dinornithiformes (moas) (**4**) belong to the neornithine subgroup called Palaeognathae ("old jaws"): mostly large, flightless birds with an "old-fashioned" type of skull. Gruiformes (cranes, rails, etc.) (**5**), Anseriformes (ducks, etc.) (**6**), Pelecaniformes (pelicans, etc.) (**7**), and Ciconiiformes (storks and New World vultures) (**8**) are in the neornithine subgroup Neognathae ("new jaws").

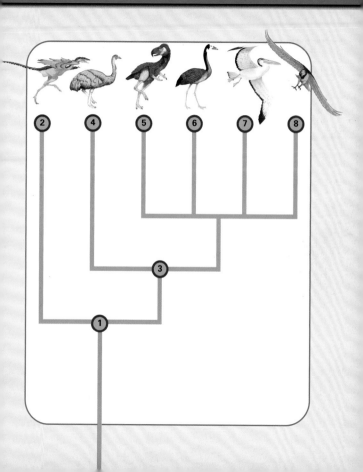

ARCHAEOPTERYX

This first known bird is also thought of as a crow-sized feathered dinosaur. Its relatives probably included the dromaeosaurs: flesh-eating theropod dinosaurs.

Archaeopteryx was a curious mixture. Like a theropod saurischian dinosaur it had sharp little teeth in long, slim jaws; a thin, flexible neck; three long, clawed fingers on each hand; a short body; long legs with stiff ankle joints; four clawed toes per foot; and a bony tail core. Like a

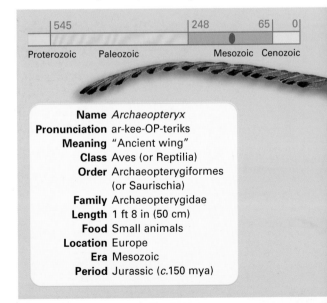

545	248	65	0
Proterozoic	Paleozoic		Mesozoic	Cenozoic

Name	*Archaeopteryx*
Pronunciation	ar-kee-OP-teriks
Meaning	"Ancient wing"
Class	Aves (or Reptilia)
Order	Archaeopterygiformes (or Saurischia)
Family	Archaeopterygidae
Length	1 ft 8 in (50 cm)
Food	Small animals
Location	Europe
Era	Mesozoic
Period	Jurassic (*c.*150 mya)

typical bird it had a covering of feathers; feathered wings; a wishbone and a shoulder girdle designed to help it fly; and small "big" toes that faced fully backward.

It might have merely fluttered weakly, but *Archaeopteryx* could also run, leap, climb, and swim. Perhaps it plucked fish from lagoons, or scavenged creatures' corpses washed up on the desert islands that it shared with the small theropod dinosaur *Compsognathus*.

DINORNIS

Giant flightless birds known as moas once roamed New Zealand. One species belonging to the genus *Dinornis* was possibly the tallest bird that ever lived. Resembling a gigantic ostrich, it grew half as heavy as a racehorse and so tall that it would have had to duck its head to step into a room with an average-height ceiling.

Proofs of its great size include immensely thick, strong thighbones far larger than an emu's. Such giant moas had thick legs and long necks, but unlike ostriches no

Name	*Dinornis*
Pronunciation	DIN-ORN-is
Meaning	"Terrible bird"
Class	Aves
Order	Dinornithiformes
Family	Dinornithidae
Height	11 ft 6 in (3.5 m)
Food	Mainly plants
Location	New Zealand
Era	Cenozoic
Period	Quaternary (1.8–0.002 mya)

545		248	65	0
Proterozoic	Paleozoic		Mesozoic	Cenozoic

wings or fused tail bones. They swallowed stones to help grind up food.

This bird was far too ponderous to fly. Anyway it had no wings. It plodded through parklike grasslands, eating seeds and fruits, and raising chicks hatched from thick-shelled eggs probably larger than an ostrich's egg. It might have survived until about 1850.

TITANIS

Titanis was one of the largest terror cranes: fierce flightless birds heavier and taller than a man. A great, deep, hooked beak like an eagle's took up most of its head which was as long as a horse's. Instead of sprouting feathers its muscular arms ended in stubby fingers tipped with vicious claws. Big, curved claws also armed the toes on its long, powerful legs.

Titanis would have lurked in long grass and dashed out to attack passing pronghorn "antelopes" or other sizable mammals. Sprinting nearly as fast as an ostrich, it delivered a

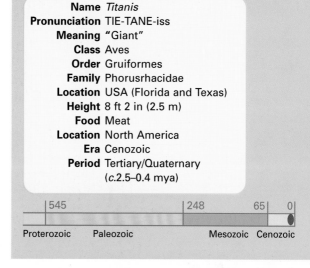

Name	*Titanis*
Pronunciation	TIE-TANE-iss
Meaning	"Giant"
Class	Aves
Order	Gruiformes
Family	Phorusrhacidae
Location	USA (Florida and Texas)
Height	8 ft 2 in (2.5 m)
Food	Meat
Location	North America
Era	Cenozoic
Period	Tertiary/Quaternary (*c.*2.5–0.4 mya)

545	248	65	0
Proterozoic	Paleozoic	Mesozoic	Cenozoic

crippling bite before the victim knew what had happened. Then *Titanis* seized and stabbed its prey with both hands, pecking and kicking to finish it off.

Though this killer bird lived in what is now Texas and Florida, its ancestors came from South America. They invaded North America after the two continents became joined.

PRESBYORNIS

If you could make a new bird out of bits of flamingo, duck, and shorebird, it might look like *Presbyornis*. This long-necked, long-legged water bird had a beak and head like a duck's, but certain skull bones resembled a flamingo's, and bones of the upper arm, lower leg, and upper foot could have been a shorebird's. Some see it as a missing link between at least two of these groups. *Presbyornis* evolved from a prehistoric shorebird and perhaps gave rise to ducks, geese, and swans.

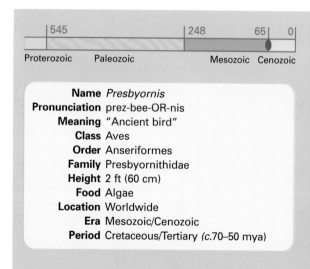

| 545 | 248 | 65 | 0 |

Proterozoic   Paleozoic   Mesozoic   Cenozoic

Name	*Presbyornis*
Pronunciation	prez-bee-OR-nis
Meaning	"Ancient bird"
Class	Aves
Order	Anseriformes
Family	Presbyornithidae
Height	2 ft (60 cm)
Food	Algae
Location	Worldwide
Era	Mesozoic/Cenozoic
Period	Cretaceous/Tertiary (*c.*70–50 mya)

Fifty million years ago vast flocks of
Presbyornis waded in hot, shallow, briny
lakes of what is now Wyoming and guzzled
the clouds of algae discoloring the salty
waters, as some flamingos do in Africa
today. Near the water's edge, it formed
great nesting colonies.

Presbyornis was so successful that it
thrived worldwide, and seems to have
persisted for many million years.

OSTEODONTORNIS

545		248	65	0
Proterozoic	Paleozoic		Mesozoic	Cenozoic

Name	*Osteodontornis*
Pronunciation	OS-tee-oh-dont-OR-nis
Meaning	"Bone-tooth bird"
Class	Aves
Order	Pelecaniformes
Family	Pelagornithidae
Wingspan	Up to 17 ft (5 m)
Food	Fish
Location	North America
Era	Cenozoic
Period	Tertiary (*c*.10–7 mya)

Imagine a giant seabird that appears part albatross part pelican. Its legs are short, its feet are webbed. Its long, strong beak is rimmed with sharp interlocking teeth. Add narrow wings long enough to span three men laid end to end and you get some idea of the largest species of *Osteodontornis*. Osteodontorns persisted for many million years, dying out about two million years ago, perhaps killed off by harsh changes in ocean climates.

The heavy-bodied seabirds glided, stiff-winged above the waves, buoyed up by a steady breeze that blew across the

sea. Now and then they swooped to pluck
a fish or squid from the water. Skewered on
their beaks' bony, toothlike spikes, the
slipperiest victims could not wriggle free.
What an *Osteodontornis* did not eat at once it
might have stored in a neck pouch rather
like a pelican's pouch. In the breeding
season it took food back to its nest, most
probably a hollow scraped out on some
low, level island.

ARGENTAVIS

Fossil finds of *Argentavis* in central Argentina revealed a flying bird bigger and heavier than anyone had thought. Some calculations suggest it stood as tall as a 12-year-old child. From beak to tail it might have matched a car for length. Quite possibly it weighed as much as a jaguar or a leopard, and its spread wings could have blocked a soccer goalmouth.

Argentavis was related to the condors and turkey vultures found in the Americas today. Like theirs its long, broad

Name *Argentavis*
Pronunciation ar-jen-TAH-vis
Meaning "Argentina bird"

wings must have been superbly shaped for soaring on warm air. Circling high up, it scanned the grassy plains below for food. Some people think it hunted small game like armadillos and rodents. But its hooked beak gaped wide enough to swallow larger prey. Perhaps it killed big flightless birds and grazing mammals, or just ate ones already dead: plunging its whole head and neck inside their corpses to gobble up the rotting meat inside.

Class Aves
Order Ciconiiformes
Family Teratornithidae
Wingspan 25 ft (7.6 m)
Food Meat
Location South America
Era Cenozoic
Period Tertiary (c.8 mya)

545		248	65	0
Proterozoic	Paleozoic		Mesozoic	Cenozoic

10. Mammals and other Synapsids

ABOUT MAMMALS AND OTHER SYNAPSIDS

The extinct mammal-like "reptiles" formed a group of backboned land animals separate from true reptiles. A hole in the skull below each eye earned mammal-like "reptiles" the name Synapsida (creatures "with arch") (**1**). Because mammals (the Mammalia) are these creatures' descendants, scientists consider mammals are synapsids too.

From early, sprawling, cold-blooded synapsids, the Pelycosauria (**2**), evolved more advanced mammal-like beasts,

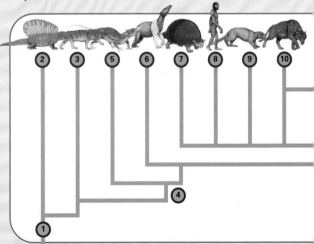

the Therapsida (**3**), which led to the Mammalia (**4**): warm-blooded backboned creatures with hair, an efficient four-chambered heart, and a sheet of muscle (the diaphragm) that helps to work the lungs. Mammal mothers produce milk for their young and most give birth instead of laying eggs. From creatures like the shrewlike Triconodonta (**5**) came today's monotremes, marsupials, and placental mammals.

This chapter describes extinct mammals from groups named in this family tree: Marsupialia (**6**), and the placental groups Xenarthra (**7**), Primates (**8**), Rodentia (**9**), Creodonta (**10**), Carnivora (**11**), Dinocerata (**12**), Litopterna (**13**), Perissodactyla (**14**), Embrithopoda (**15**), Proboscidea (**16**), Artiodactyla (**17**), Mesonychia (**18**), and Cetacea (**19**).

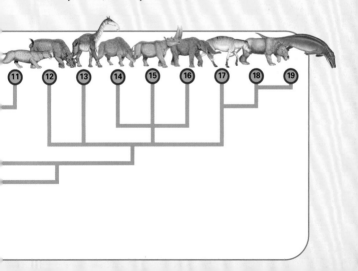

EDAPHOSAURUS

Edaphosaurus belonged to the pelycosaurs, a group of reptile-like synapsids. This mammal-like "reptile" had a large, low-slung body, and a skin sail on its back, supported by long bony spines with little crossbars, rising from its vertebrae. Perhaps individuals recognized each other by their sails, or perhaps the sails controlled body temperature in the way this book suggests for *Edaphosaurus*'s most dangerous enemy, *Dimetrodon*.

Name	*Edaphosaurus*
Pronunciation	I-DAF-oh-SORE-us
Meaning	"Earth lizard"
Class	Synapsida
Order	Pelycosauria
Family	Edaphosauridae
Length	10 ft (3 m)
Food	Perhaps plants and animals
Location	Europe and North America
Era	Paleozoic
Period	Permian (*c.*280–260 mya)

For the body's size the head seems tiny, yet its lower jaw was deep and strong. Small, peglike teeth rimmed the jaws and formed "pavements" in the mouth roof and the inside of the lower jaw. *Edaphosaurus* might have used these teeth to eat soft plants, a bulky food digested in its roomy gut. Some scientists see the teeth as crushers, and believe they crunched up little shellfish living in shallow pools and rivers. Perhaps the creature's food consisted of mixed mouthfuls of small animals and water plants.

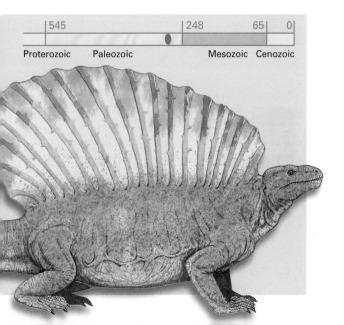

545		248	65	0
Proterozoic	Paleozoic		Mesozoic	Cenozoic

DIMETRODON

A tall skin sail on its back and jaws with dagger-like teeth were hallmarks of this big four-legged beast on the evolutionary line that led to mammals. *Dimetrodon* was one of the first backboned land animals powerful enough to kill creatures as large as itself.

The car-length top predator *Dimetrodon* terrorised its plant-eating synapsid relatives. When its long, narrow jaws gaped wide

Name	*Dimetrodon*
Pronunciation	die-MET-roe-don
Meaning	"Two-measure tooth"
Class	Synapsida
Order	Pelycosauria
Family	Sphenacodontidae
Length	11 ft 6 in (3.5 m)

they bared big, stabbing canines for piercing, and sharp teeth for biting and grasping.

The sail held up by tall bony rods from its backbone perhaps helped hunting. If *Dimetrodon* was cold-blooded, standing sideways to the morning sun heated its sail that then warmed the rest of its body. *Dimetrodon* would have become active while reptiles without sails were still too cold and sluggish to escape. To avoid overheating at midday it turned its back to the sun.

Food	Meat
Location	North America, Europe
Era	Paleozoic
Period	Permian (*c.*280–270 mya)

545		248	65	0
Proterozoic	Paleozoic		Mesozoic	Cenozoic

MOSCHOPS

A synapsid plant-eater as strong as a small truck, *Moschops* suggests a creature cobbled together from different species of animal of varying sizes. Its short, domed head, small hands and feet, and brief tail seem too tiny for its thick neck and the great barrel-shaped body with a back sloping steeply down like a giraffe's. The sturdy muscular hindlimbs seem a poor match for the massive front limbs, for although *Moschops* held its hind limbs erect its elbows stuck out to the sides.

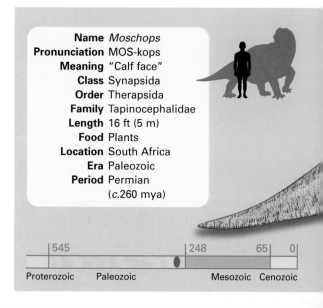

Name	*Moschops*
Pronunciation	MOS-kops
Meaning	"Calf face"
Class	Synapsida
Order	Therapsida
Family	Tapinocephalidae
Length	16 ft (5 m)
Food	Plants
Location	South Africa
Era	Paleozoic
Period	Permian
	(*c.*260 mya)

545		248	65	0
Proterozoic	Paleozoic		Mesozoic	Cenozoic

The animal used its chisel-shaped teeth for chopping up plant foods. Rival males probably employed their thick skulls and strong necks and shoulders in head-butting contests, much as mountain sheep do today.

Moschops belonged to the dinocephalians ("terrible heads"). These formed part of an advanced group of synapsids known as therapsids ("mammal arches").

LYCAENOPS

"Wolf face" was a rangy, sharp-fanged predator the size of a large dog. It belonged to those therapsids called gorgonopsians (in Greek mythology the Gorgons were terrible sisters whose glance turned people to stone).

Lycaenops probably hunted in packs. By attacking as a team, a group of these fairly small killers could bring down a plant-eating therapsid several times their own size. African hunting dogs use this technique to bring down a wildebeest. Thick hide

Name	*Lycaenops*
Pronunciation	Lie-KINE-ops
Meaning	"Wolf face"
Class	Synapsida

545		248	65	0
Proterozoic	Paleozoic		Mesozoic	Cenozoic

gave little protection for creatures like *Moschops*. Leaping onto its back, *Lycaenops* opened its jaws so wide they formed a right angle, baring rows of long, pointed teeth. Two great daggerlike canines jutted down like those of a sabre-toothed cat. *Lycaenops* sank its fangs in the *Moschops*'s neck until the teeth interlocked. Then it tore out a mouthful of flesh. Weakened by loss of blood, the victim collapsed and would be quickly devoured by the pack.

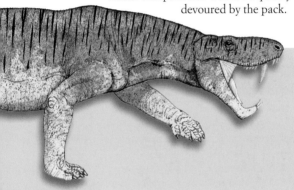

Order	Therapsida
Family	Gorgonopsidae
Length	3 ft 3 in (1 m)
Food	Meat
Location	South Africa
Era	Paleozoic
Period	Permian (*c.*260 mya)

LYSTROSAURUS

Squat, stocky *Lystrosaurus* rather resembled a thick-legged pig with erect hind limbs and elbows sticking out at the sides. Its short, steep head featured big eye sockets, nostrils high up, just ahead of the eyes, and strong, beaked jaws, toothless except for two long canine teeth forming short tusks jutting down from the upper jaw. Teeth like this earned such therapsid synapsids the name of *dicynodonts* ("two dog teeth").

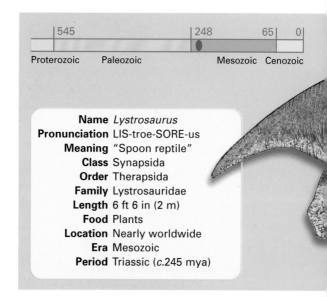

	545		248	65	0
Proterozoic	Paleozoic		Mesozoic	Cenozoic	

Name *Lystrosaurus*
Pronunciation LIS-troe-SORE-us
Meaning "Spoon reptile"
Class Synapsida
Order Therapsida
Family Lystrosauridae
Length 6 ft 6 in (2 m)
Food Plants
Location Nearly worldwide
Era Mesozoic
Period Triassic (*c.*245 mya)

Lystrosaurus's horny beak chopped up leaves and stems with help from strong muscles producing fore-and-aft jaw movements. Its high-level eyes have led some people to suppose it chomped on water plants while wallowing in lakes like a hippopotamus. More likely it lived on dry land. The most successful and widespread of all mammal-like "reptiles," *Lystrosaurus* inhabited Africa, Asia, Antarctica, and Europe, and its fossils outnumber those of all other sizable creatures from the same time.

CYNOGNATHUS

Cynognathus could almost be mistaken for a powerful, wolf-sized dog, with long, strong jaws and sharp teeth.

Like their mammal descendants, such cynodont therapsids walked with hind limbs tucked under a body with a well-defined chest and lower back, probably separated by a muscular sheet called a diaphragm that helped to fill and empty the lungs. The mouth's design

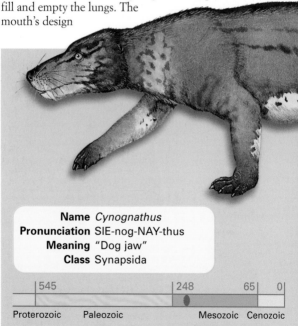

Name	*Cynognathus*
Pronunciation	SIE-nog-NAY-thus
Meaning	"Dog jaw"
Class	Synapsida

545		248	65	0
Proterozoic	Paleozoic		Mesozoic	Cenozoic

allowed breathing while eating, and whisker pits in skull snouts suggest cynodonts were hairy. All this hints at warm-blooded beasts with internal temperature control.

The muscular jaws gaped wide and bit hard, with short, sharp incisors for nipping and cutting, long, pointed canines for stabbing, and many-pointed cheek teeth for slicing and shearing. Each side of the long, lower jaw had one large, strong dentary bone as in mammals, plus traces of bones now in the middle ears of mammals.

Order	Therapsida
Family	Cynognathidae
Length	3 ft 3 in (1 m)
Food	Meat
Location	South Africa, South America
Era	Mesozoic
Period	Triassic (*c.*230 mya)

MEGAZOSTRODON

Mouse-sized *Megazostrodon* was a very early mammal which looked much like a modern shrew. Its fossil bones and teeth were different enough from those of its therapsid ancestors for many scientists to believe that this tiny animal had been furry and warm-blooded, and that the mothers suckled their young.

Inside its skull, tiny bones derived from the lower jawbones of a therapsid ancestor helped its hearing. Then, too, the

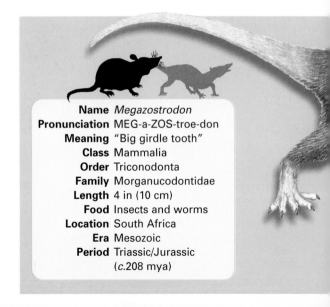

Name	*Megazostrodon*
Pronunciation	MEG-a-ZOS-troe-don
Meaning	"Big girdle tooth"
Class	Mammalia
Order	Triconodonta
Family	Morganucodontidae
Length	4 in (10 cm)
Food	Insects and worms
Location	South Africa
Era	Mesozoic
Period	Triassic/Jurassic (*c.*208 mya)

creature seems to have grown first and second sets of teeth, as modern mammals do. However, its limbs stuck out somewhat to the sides instead of straight down like those of shrews and mice.

As *Megazostrodon* scuttled around, its long, sensitive shrewlike snout sniffed out insects and worms, crunched up by its four kinds of sharp little teeth. This little hunter probably ran around at night, and slept by day inside a burrow, safe from hungry dinosaurs.

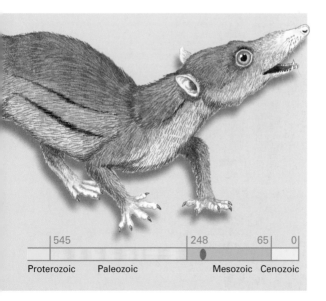

545		248	65	0
Proterozoic	Paleozoic		Mesozoic	Cenozoic

PALORCHESTES

Swamp monsters called bunyips might be folk memories of
Palorchestes, the weirdest beast that ever roamed Australia.
First mistaken for a kangaroo, its fossils really came from a
very different kind of marsupial (pouched mammal).

As big as a bull, the largest species had massive arms with
strong, sharp finger claws. Its hind limbs seem to have
been less powerful but each foot bore four claws. The tail
was short. The strangest feature was its narrow head,
which evidently ended in a rubbery trunk.

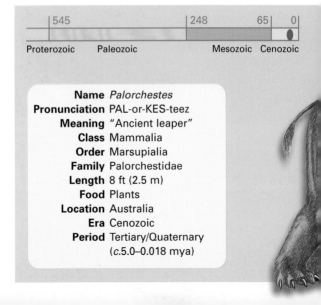

545		248	65	0
Proterozoic	Paleozoic		Mesozoic	Cenozoic

Name	*Palorchestes*
Pronunciation	PAL-or-KES-teez
Meaning	"Ancient leaper"
Class	Mammalia
Order	Marsupialia
Family	Palorchestidae
Length	8 ft (2.5 m)
Food	Plants
Location	Australia
Era	Cenozoic
Period	Tertiary/Quaternary (*c.*5.0–0.018 mya)

Palorchestes was probably Australia's equivalent of the giant ground sloths of America. Walking with its big claws retracted like a cat's (or perhaps on its knuckles), *Palorchestes* reared to rip off tree bark with its claws. Curling its trunk and long, thin tongue around leafy twigs, it pulled these into its mouth. There, high-crowned molars ground the leaves and bark to pulp.

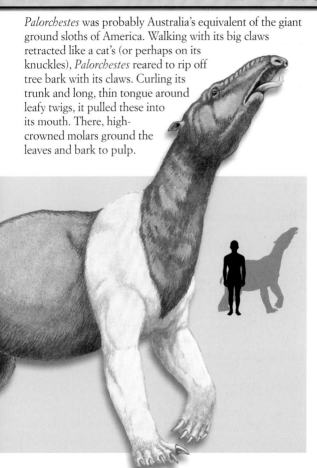

THYLACOLEO

"Pouched lion" was Australia's marsupial equivalent of the big cats found in other continents.

This leopard-sized killer had a short, somewhat catlike face, long limbs, and paws equipped with powerful claws. The huge thumbs, capable of grasping, bore great retractable claws. Instead of long stabbing canine teeth like a cat's there were just small pegs, but dangerously jutting sharp incisors, and the enlarged third premolars formed

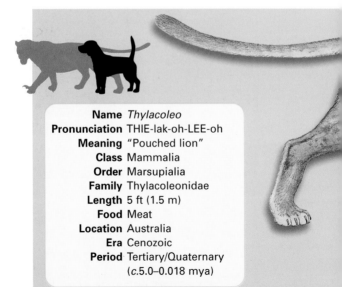

Name	*Thylacoleo*
Pronunciation	THIE-lak-oh-LEE-oh
Meaning	"Pouched lion"
Class	Mammalia
Order	Marsupialia
Family	Thylacoleonidae
Length	5 ft (1.5 m)
Food	Meat
Location	Australia
Era	Cenozoic
Period	Tertiary/Quaternary (*c.*5.0–0.018 mya)

long, tall blades shaped to shear through meat as easily as scissors slice their way through sheets of paper.

Thylacoleo preyed on kangaroos and wombats. Clutching a victim with its forepaws, it stabbed the throat with its incisors and probably hung on until the victim died of suffocation. Incisors and premolars then stripped and sliced off flesh. After eating all it could, *Thylacoleo* might have hauled its prey into a tree: a larder, safe from scavengers. Leopards do the same today.

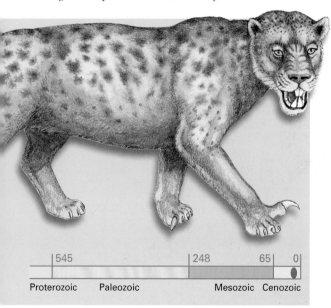

545			248	65	0
Proterozoic	Paleozoic			Mesozoic	Cenozoic

GLYPTODON

The best-protected mammal ever must be this prehistoric relative of the armadillos that live in the Americas today. As tall as a pony and as long as a small car, *Glyptodon* looked like a colossal tortoise or a living battle tank.

Horn-sheathed bony plates formed a domed shell above its high, curved back. A bony skullcap crowned its short, deep head. Even its tail was ringed with spiky bones. The whole suit of armor weighed as much as a horse, but it protected

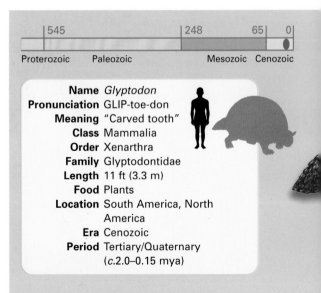

	545		248	65	0
	Proterozoic	Paleozoic		Mesozoic	Cenozoic

Name *Glyptodon*
Pronunciation GLIP-toe-don
Meaning "Carved tooth"
Class Mammalia
Order Xenarthra
Family Glyptodontidae
Length 11 ft (3.3 m)
Food Plants
Location South America, North America
Era Cenozoic
Period Tertiary/Quaternary (*c.*2.0–0.15 mya)

Glyptodon from big, catlike marsupial carnivores and big cats, both armed with canine "sabres."

Fused spinal bones and short, thick limbs held up its heavy load as *Glyptodon* scratched for roots and tubers with its hoof-shaped claws, and crunched them with its strong cheek teeth. The front of its mouth was toothless. Like armadillos, sloths and anteaters, it belonged to the placental mammals known as *edentates* ("animals without teeth").

AUSTRALOPITHECUS

Three million years ago two groups of creatures that seemed half ape, half human were evolving on Africa's plains. One group of these australopithecines or "southern apes" had massive jaws for chewing tough plant foods. Another group had smaller jaws. Both groups were lightly built.

Best known of the second group is *Australopithecus afarensis,* from Ethiopia's Afar region. No bigger than a six-year-old child, one female skeleton nicknamed Lucy revealed a mix of ape and human features. Like humans

545		248	65	0
Proterozoic	Paleozoic		Mesozoic	Cenozoic

Name	*Australopithecus*
Pronunciation	os-TRAL-oh-PITH-e-kus
Meaning	"Southern ape"
Class	Mammalia
Order	Primates
Family	Hominidae
Height	3 ft 3 in–5 ft 3 in (1.0–1.6 m)
Food	Plants and meat
Location	Africa
Era	Cenozoic
Period	Tertiary/Quaternary (*c.*4.1–1.5 mya)

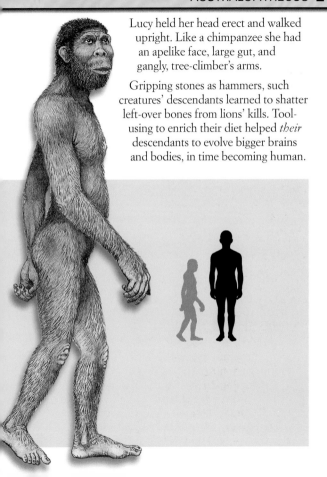

Lucy held her head erect and walked upright. Like a chimpanzee she had an apelike face, large gut, and gangly, tree-climber's arms.

Gripping stones as hammers, such creatures' descendants learned to shatter left-over bones from lions' kills. Tool-using to enrich their diet helped *their* descendants to evolve bigger brains and bodies, in time becoming human.

CASTOROIDES

A rodent as big as a black bear and almost as heavy as three average men roamed North America in the last Ice Age. *Castoroides* was six times heavier and more than twice as long as the living beavers it resembled.

Like today's beavers, this burly mammal swam by kicking water backward with its webbed hind feet, and used its stiff, flat, scaly tail to steer. Self-sharpening, chisel-

Name	*Castoroides*
Pronunciation	KAS-tor-OYD-eez
Meaning	"Beaver-like" [creature]
Class	Mammalia
Order	Rodentia
Family	Castoridae

shaped incisor teeth the length of dinner-knife blades enabled it to gnaw through wood and chop down trees and saplings. Beside or in a swamp, *Castoroides* built its lodge: a heap of saplings with a living-chamber inside. Unlike today's North American beavers, it did not dam streams to create pools with island lodges.

More than 100,000 years ago *Castoroides* spread north through lakes to beyond the Arctic Circle, but it died out as the Ice Age ended about 10,000 years ago.

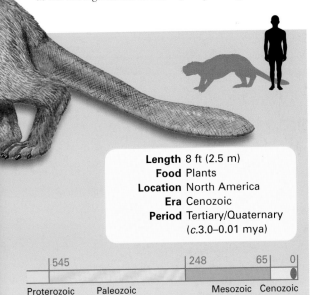

Length	8 ft (2.5 m)
Food	Plants
Location	North America
Era	Cenozoic
Period	Tertiary/Quaternary (*c*.3.0–0.01 mya)

545			248	65	0
Proterozoic	Paleozoic			Mesozoic	Cenozoic

MEGISTOTHERIUM

Megistotherium was one of the largest-ever flesh-eating land mammals, with a head three times the size of a lion's. It belonged to the creodonts ("flesh teeth" creatures), a major group of prehistoric carnivores.

Although this hunter had clawed toes, its major weapons were its jaws and teeth. Behind the narrow snout, the skull's sides flared out in bony arches to make room for immensely powerful jaw muscles. When *Megistotherium*

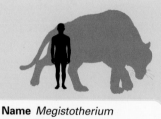

Name	*Megistotherium*
Pronunciation	MEG-is-toe-THEE-ri-um
Meaning	"Very big beast"
Class	Mammalia
Order	Creodonta
Family	Hyaenodontidae
Length	13 ft (4 m)
Food	Meat
Location	North Africa
Era	Cenozoic
Period	Tertiary (*c.*23–20 mya)

bit into meaty prey, its long canine fangs pierced the victim's hide, and sharp-crowned top and bottom cheek teeth meshed together, slicing through thick flesh as easily as scissors cut through paper.

Big plant-eating mammals were its most likely victims. *Megistotherium* might have tackled even mastodonts. Some of these prehistoric relatives of elephants lived at the same time and place (present-day Libya) as is creodont.

545		248	65	0
Proterozoic	Paleozoic		Mesozoic	Cenozoic

SMILODON

Smilodon was a large cat with a short tail, strong neck, and powerful shoulders. Two long upper canine teeth like curved sword blades fitted outside the lower jaw when this was closed. This carnivore was one of the last of a variety of prehistoric cats with swordlike teeth.

Sabre-toothed cats are also known as stabbing cats from the way they tackled thick-skinned prey. Fairly short-limbed and unable to run fast, they chose large,

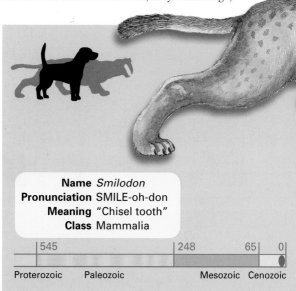

Name	*Smilodon*
Pronunciation	SMILE-oh-don
Meaning	"Chisel tooth"
Class	Mammalia

545		248	65	0
Proterozoic	Paleozoic		Mesozoic	Cenozoic

slow-moving victims such as elephants and giant ground sloths. Leaping, jaws wide open, upon a young individual, *Smilodon* stabbed through its hide then closed its mouth and tore out a lump of meat.

Thousands of *Smilodon* skeletons have been discovered in Los Angeles' natural tar pools. Attracted by the cries of creatures trapped while drinking rainwater lying on the surface, the cats, too, became stuck in the tar below.

Order	Carnivora
Family	Felidae
Length	4 ft (1.2 m)
Food	Meat
Location	North America and South America
Era	Cenozoic
Period	Tertiary/Quaternary (*c.*2.0–0.01 mya)

UINTATHERIUM

Uintatherium was one of the first big mammals: a plant-eater the size of a large rhinoceros, with a heavy body, thick limbs and short, splayed toes tipped by broad, hooflike nails. Found in Colorado's Uinta Mountains, it gave its name to the uintatheres, a group of primitive hoofed mammals that once lived in North America and Asia.

Bizarre knobbly heads earned uintatheres their scientific name

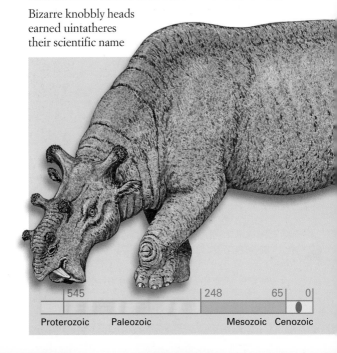

545		248	65	0
Proterozoic	Paleozoic		Mesozoic	Cenozoic

Dinocerata (creatures with "terrible horns"). *Uintatherium*'s grotesque head sprouted six blunt, bony knobs: two little knobs on the snout tip, two taller knobs in front of the eyes, and two large knobs above and behind the eyes. Males also grew wickedly long upper canine teeth.

Uintatherium browsed at the edges of woods where its low-crowned cheek teeth would have chewed soft-leaved plants. In the mating season, rival males perhaps butted heads and slashed one another with their canine tusks.

Name	*Uintatherium*
Pronunciation	YOU-in-ta-THEE-ri-um
Meaning	"Uinta beast"
Class	Mammalia
Order	Dinocerata
Family	Uintatheriidae
Length	11 ft (3.5 m)
Food	Plants
Location	North America and Asia
Era	Cenozoic
Period	Tertiary (*c.*45–40 mya)

MACRAUCHENIA

Macrauchenia looked like a creature made from parts of at least three others. Its small head and long neck and limbs gave it the general shape of a camel. Its three-toed feet tipped with small hooves somewhat resembled the feet of a rhinoceros. The high nostril opening in its skull between the eye sockets hints at a flexible trunk a bit like an elephant's but much shorter.

545	248	65	0

Proterozoic | Paleozoic | Mesozoic | Cenozoic

Name	*Macrauchenia*
Pronunciation	mak-roe-KEEN-ia
Meaning	"Long-necked"
Class	Mammalia
Order	Litopterna
Family	Macraucheniidae
Length	10 ft (3 m)
Food	Plants
Location	South America
Era	Cenozoic
Period	Quaternary (c.1–0.01 mya)

Macrauchenia probably browsed on soft-leafed shrubs and trees. Raising its head and craning its neck it would have curled its trunk around tender leafy sprays high above the ground and pulled these into its mouth to be chewed by its low-crowned cheek teeth.

This strange mammal belonged to the litopterns (creatures with "smooth heel-bones"), hoofed mammals resembling camels or horses but not closely related to either. Litopterns flourished in South America when it was an island.

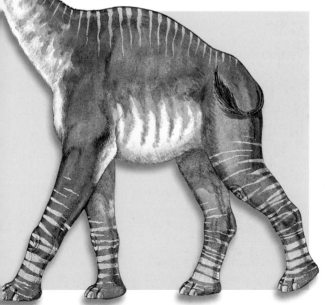

HYRACOTHERIUM

Hyracotherium was the earliest known horse, a beast no bigger than a fox. Its curved back resembled a tapir's. Its head was longer in relation to its body than a modern horse's, and its jaws contained more teeth. Today's horses have tall teeth for chewing tough grasses; *Hyracotherium*'s low-crowned teeth could only chew soft-leaved forest plants.

Perhaps the most striking differences between this and a

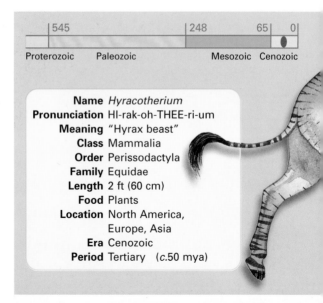

	545		248	65	0
Proterozoic	Paleozoic			Mesozoic	Cenozoic

Name *Hyracotherium*
Pronunciation HI-rak-oh-THEE-ri-um
Meaning "Hyrax beast"
Class Mammalia
Order Perissodactyla
Family Equidae
Length 2 ft (60 cm)
Food Plants
Location North America, Europe, Asia
Era Cenozoic
Period Tertiary (*c.*50 mya)

modern horse involved the feet. A living horse's foot consists of a single large hoofed toe. *Hyracotherium* had three small toes on each hind foot and four toes on each forefoot, each toe supported by a fleshy pad. As grasslands replaced forests, such small, shy woodland browsers evolved into the long-legged, fleet-footed grazing horses of today. Meanwhile their side toes shrank and disappeared. Now horses are the only plentiful survivors of that once numerous group of odd toed ungulates (hoofed mammals) called perissodactyls.

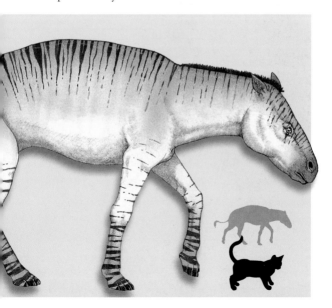

BRONTOTHERIUM

This relative of the horses and rhinoceroses was built rather like an immense rhinoceros, with room-high shoulders and a massive body, supported by thick legs and broad, short feet. Each forefoot bore four hoofed toes and there were three toes on each hindfoot.

The thick neck's powerful muscles supported a heavy head whose low snout bore the monster's strangest feature: a tall, blunt, bony

Y-shaped horn that stuck up like some gigantic catapult.
Males very probably brandished their horns to impress
females or each other. Perhaps rival males also met head-on
in shoving contests.

Brontotherium roamed woodland glades of North America
east of the Rocky Mountains. Its teeth were suitable for
cropping and chewing shrubs and bushy trees. When these
soft-leaved plants gave way to abrasive grasses
Brontotherium became extinct.

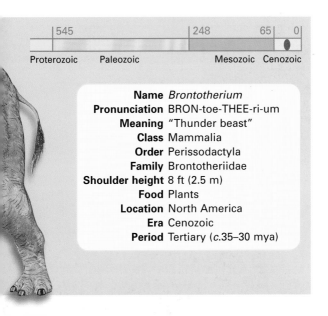

	545		248	65	0
Proterozoic		Paleozoic		Mesozoic	Cenozoic

Name	*Brontotherium*
Pronunciation	BRON-toe-THEE-ri-um
Meaning	"Thunder beast"
Class	Mammalia
Order	Perissodactyla
Family	Brontotheriidae
Shoulder height	8 ft (2.5 m)
Food	Plants
Location	North America
Era	Cenozoic
Period	Tertiary (*c.*35–30 mya)

CHALICOTHERIUM

At first glance, *Chalicotherium* looked like a horse. Yet while its head resembled a modern horse's head, its low-crowned cheek-teeth could not have chewed up tough grass. Then, too, its long forelimbs remind us of a gorilla's long, strong arms, and its back sloped steeply down from high shoulders to low hindquarters with broad hips like those of the big, extinct ground sloths. Among its least horselike features were each limb's three toes tipped with curved claws.

545		248	65	0
Proterozoic	Paleozoic		Mesozoic	Cenozoic

Name	*Chalicotherium*
Pronunciation	KAL-i-koe-THEE-ri-um
Meaning	"Pebble beast"
Class	Mammalia
Order	Perissodactyla
Family	Chalicotheriidae
Length	10 ft (3 m)
Food	Plants
Location	Europe, Asia, Africa
Era	Cenozoic
Period	Tertiary (*c.*16–6 mya)

Chalicotherium seems to have walked on its knuckles, much as gorillas do. For feeding it probably sat on its haunches, or reared. Perhaps it hooked leafy branches down to its mouth. This way it could have reached leaves 13 feet (4 m) off the ground. However, scientists suspect that its elbows could not bend enough to make this a regular habit. Other possible uses for its claws were digging up edible roots or fending off enemies.

INDRICOTHERIUM

This hornless rhinoceros was probably the most colossal land mammal of all time. One estimate makes it two and a half times the weight of an African bull elephant. Another puts it twice as heavy as that. Built like a giant horse, this high-level browser stood taller than a giraffe. If it was alive now it could peer into an upstairs window.

Supporting its great body were strong spinal bones scooped out rather like a

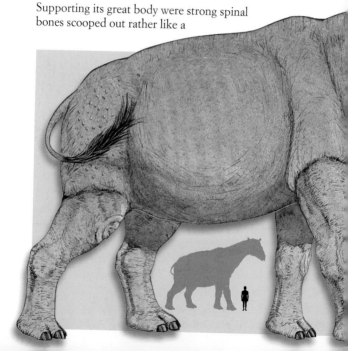

sauropod dinosaur's to cut down weight, and pillarlike legs with three-toed feet. *Indricotherium* craned its long neck to nibble treetop leaves. Its rubbery upper lip and jutting lower front teeth would have helped to bring food to its mouth, for strongly ridged cheek teeth to grind to a pulp.

This immense mammal evolved from small, lightly built, agile rhinoceroses the shape and size of ponies.

Name	*Indricotherium*
Pronunciation	IN-dri-koe-THEE-ri-um
Meaning	"Indra [a god] image beast"
Class	Mammalia
Order	Perissodactyla
Family	Hyracodontidae
Length	26 ft (8 m)
Food	Plants
Location	Asia and Europe
Era	Cenozoic
Period	Tertiary (*c.*25 mya)

545		248	65	0
Proterozoic	Paleozoic		Mesozoic	Cenozoic

ARSINOITHERIUM

Two hollow horns as long as its head sprouted side by side from the face of this African mammal as big as a large rhinoceros. The horns' bases covered most of its face between nostrils and eyes. Above the eyes rose two small bony knobs, probably covered in skin.

Arsinoitherium had a large head, a deep, broad body, and thick limbs like an elephant's. The short, spreading toes ended in blunt nails shaped as little hooves. This weird beast's ridged, high-crowned cheek teeth ground up tough vegetation better than the teeth of most other early plant-eating mammals. Perhaps it munched coarse-leaved plants in swamp forests. If a rival or a mesonychid or creodont ventured too near, it brandished its horns.

Scientists place *Arsinoitherium* and similar animals in a group called embrithopods. These strange mammals are probably related to the elephants.

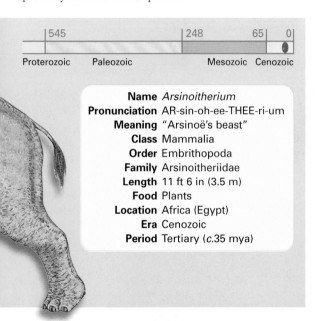

	545		248	65	0
Proterozoic		Paleozoic		Mesozoic	Cenozoic

Name *Arsinoitherium*
Pronunciation AR-sin-oh-ee-THEE-ri-um
Meaning "Arsinoë's beast"
Class Mammalia
Order Embrithopoda
Family Arsinoitheriidae
Length 11 ft 6 in (3.5 m)
Food Plants
Location Africa (Egypt)
Era Cenozoic
Period Tertiary (*c.*35 mya)

PLATYBELODON

Platybelodon resembled an outlandish-looking elephant with a flattened trunk and four tusks. Two upper canine teeth formed short tusks jutting down from its upper jaw, and two long incisor teeth formed wide, flat, blunt tusks jutting forwards from its elongated lower jaw.

Scientists believe this creature used its spade-shaped tusks to scoop up water plants or dig plants from bogs, then used its trunk to push this food into its mouth.

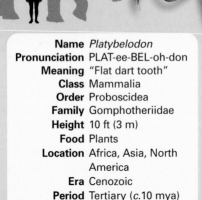

Name	*Platybelodon*
Pronunciation	PLAT-ee-BEL-oh-don
Meaning	"Flat dart tooth"
Class	Mammalia
Order	Proboscidea
Family	Gomphotheriidae
Height	10 ft (3 m)
Food	Plants
Location	Africa, Asia, North America
Era	Cenozoic
Period	Tertiary (c.10 mya)

Such so-called shovel tuskers were one of many prehistoric types of proboscidean: trunked mammals related to the living elephants. Shovel tuskers belonged to the mastodonts: a group of big, heavy-bodied quadrupeds with a short, thick neck, pillarlike legs, and cheek teeth crowned by several pairs of rounded mound-shaped cusps, not ridged and grooved across like the immense cheek teeth of a modern elephant.

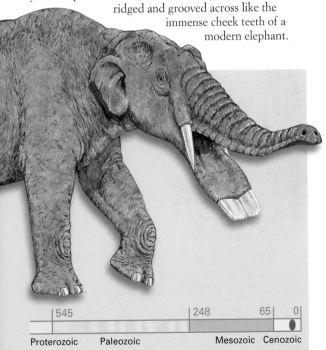

545		248	65	0
Proterozoic	Paleozoic		Mesozoic	Cenozoic

SYNTHETOCERAS

Males of this hoofed mammal had a horn made of two fused horns jutting up from its long, slender snout. High up the two split apart, forming a V-shaped bony prong. Two shorter, curved horns rose from the animal's brows. A deer sheds and regrows its antlers each year, but *Synthetoceras*'s horns had to last it for life.

Herds of this mammal grazed the prairies of Texas. In the breeding season, males probably brandished

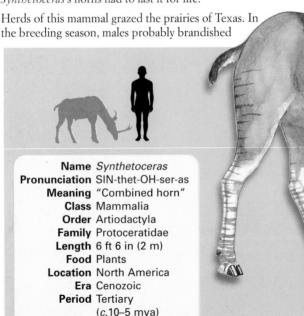

Name	*Synthetoceras*
Pronunciation	SIN-thet-OH-ser-as
Meaning	"Combined horn"
Class	Mammalia
Order	Artiodactyla
Family	Protoceratidae
Length	6 ft 6 in (2 m)
Food	Plants
Location	North America
Era	Cenozoic
Period	Tertiary (*c.*10–5 mya)

their horns to impress females. Maybe rival males clashed horns like two swordsmen fencing. If a large carnivore threatened, their long legs provided a quick getaway.

Synthetoceras is pictured like a deer but it might have been stockier. It was closely related to camels. Like deer, camels, and cattle, such cud-chewing grazers were artiodactyls: even-toed hoofed mammals. Artiodactyls now far outnumber the odd-toed horse and its kin.

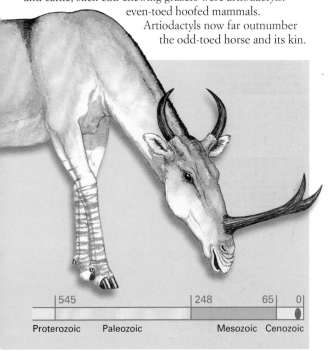

545		248	65	0
Proterozoic	Paleozoic		Mesozoic	Cenozoic

MEGALOCEROS

Apart from its great size, immense, spreading antlers were this giant deer's most obvious hallmark. At 11 feet 6 inches (3.5 m) across they were as wide as some small cars are long and immensely heavy. Only males had this huge headgear, which they shed and regrew each year. To get enough of the right ingredients for building new antlers they must have eaten huge amounts of calcium-rich food.

Besides cropping calcium-rich plants perhaps they gnawed shed antlers found lying around on the ground.

Megaloceros herds roamed Europe and Asia during the Ice Age. Remains of dozens of individuals have turned up in Ireland. These finds helped to earn this largest of all the known deer its popular name Irish elk (elk meaning moose).

In fact its closest living relative is not that big wild deer but the fallow deer, a much smaller species kept in many parks and zoos. *Megaloceros* itself died out at least 2,500 years ago.

Name	*Megaloceros*
Pronunciation	MEG-al-OH-ser-os
Meaning	"Big horn"
Class	Mammalia
Order	Artiodactyla
Family	Cervidae
Length	8 ft (2.5 m)
Food	Plants
Location	Europe, Asia, North Africa
Era	Cenozoic
Period	Quaternary (*c.*1.5–0.002 mya)

545	248	65	0
Proterozoic Paleozoic		Mesozoic	Cenozoic

ANDREWSARCHUS

No known meat-eating land mammal matched this beast for size. Its 2-foot-11-inch (83 cm) skull is the only evidence we have, but it outstrips *Megistotherium*'s great skull by 7 inches (18 cm) so the owner must have been immense.

Some people believe that *Andrewsarchus* resembled a gigantic bear. Others picture it as an outsize, long-headed hyena. Either way it was probably too ponderous to chase

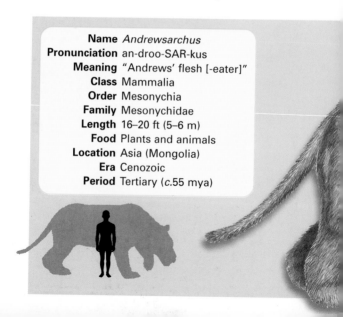

Name	*Andrewsarchus*
Pronunciation	an-droo-SAR-kus
Meaning	"Andrews' flesh [-eater]"
Class	Mammalia
Order	Mesonychia
Family	Mesonychidae
Length	16–20 ft (5–6 m)
Food	Plants and animals
Location	Asia (Mongolia)
Era	Cenozoic
Period	Tertiary (*c.*55 mya)

big game. Most likely *Andrewsarchus* ate any animals or edible plants that came its way, using its big, blunt-cusped cheek teeth to crunch the bones of creatures it found already dead.

Andrewsarchus belonged to the mesonychids ("intermediate clawed beasts"): prehistoric carnivores related to today's plant-eating "even-toed" hoofed mammals and the whales. Indeed *Andrewsarchus*'s long skull and cheek teeth with distinctive cusps look very like an early whale's.

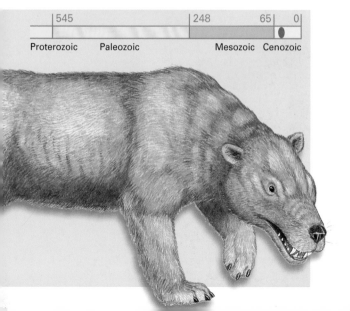

	545		248	65	0
Proterozoic		Paleozoic		Mesozoic	Cenozoic

AMBULOCETUS

Named "the walking whale that swam," *Ambulocetus* is a missing link between prehistoric land mammals and their descendants the whales which cannot leave the sea.

This proto-whale was as big as a large sea lion. Its limbs were longer than a sea lion's but too short for moving fast on land, and its forelimbs sprawled out to the sides. It swam by kicking water backward with

Name	*Ambulocetus*
Pronunciation	amb-you-loe-SEE-tus
Meaning	"Walking whale"
Class	Mammalia
Order	Cetacea
Family	Ambulocetidae
Length	10 ft (3 m)
Food	Fish and perhaps meat
Location	Pakistan
Era	Cenozoic
Period	Tertiary (*c.*50 mya)

its webbed hind feet. Because its backbone was still fused to its hipbones *Ambulocetus* could not swim by making its body undulate up and down like a limbless whale.

Ambulocetus hunted in shallow seas and rivers, catching fish in long jaws with sharklike teeth like those of the land-bound mesonychids. Perhaps such prehistoric meat-eaters were its ancestors. Yet certain biochemicals in living whales suggest that these share a common ancestor with the hoofed, plant-eating hippopotamuses.

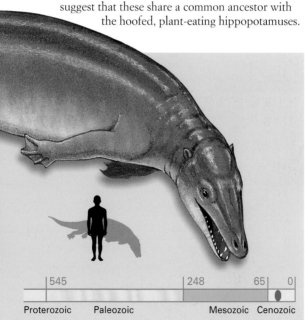

545			248	65	0
Proterozoic	Paleozoic			Mesozoic	Cenozoic

Glossary

Abdomen Belly; also the rear part of an insect or spider.

Acanthodii/Acanthodians Extinct spiny-finned fishes.

Actinopterygians Ray-finned osteichthyans.

Aeon The largest geological time unit, divided into eras.

Aetosaurs Extinct plant-eating thecodonts.

Ammonites Extinct cephalopods, most living in a coiled shell and swimming at various depths in the sea.

Amniotes Tetrapods producing eggs that develop out of water. They include reptiles, birds, and mammals.

Amphibians Tetrapods that lay eggs in water.

Anapsids Reptiles with a primitive type of skull.

Archaea Tiny, primitive, one-celled organisms with no cell nucleus. See also *Bacteria*.

Archosaurs "Ruling reptiles": a group including dinosaurs, pterosaurs, and crocodilians.

Arthropods Jointed-legged invertebrates.

Artiodactyls The "even-toed" hoofed mammals.

Australopithecines Extinct "ape men."

Bacteria One of two groups of tiny, one-celled organisms with no cell nucleus. Some cause diseases.

Birds Feathered tetrapods with arms evolved as wings.

Bivalves Molluscs with a hinged shell.

Brachiopods Creatures resembling bivalve molluscs.

Carapace A type of shell protecting a body.

Carnivores Meat-eaters, especially mammals including dogs, cats, and their relatives.

Cells The tiny building blocks of every living thing.

Cephalopods Many-armed molluscs.

Chondrichthyes Sharks and their relatives.

Chordates Animals reinforced internally by a notochord at some stage in their lives.

Clade A group of living things with the same ancestor.

Cladistics Classifying living things by clades.

Class A group of related orders.

Conodonts Extinct, open-mouthed, eel-like creatures.

Creodonts A group of extinct flesh-eating mammals.

Diapsids Reptiles with two skull holes behind the eye.

Dicynodonts A group of plant-eating therapsids.

Dinocephalians A group of carnivorous therapsids.

Dinosaurs A great, long-lived group of two-legged and four-legged plant-eating and carnivorous archosaurs with erect limbs. Many were large or immense.

Dromaeosaurs Fierce but lightly built theropods.

Echinoderms Starfishes, sea urchins and their relatives.

Edentates Armadillos, sloths, and their relatives.

Embrithopods Extinct rhinoceros-like mammals.

Era A geological time unit made up of periods.

Eukaryotes Living things whose cells have a nucleus.

Family A group of related genera.

Fishes Aquatic vertebrates with gills and fins.

Fossil Remains or traces of a prehistoric organism.

Genus A group of related species.

Gorgonopsians A group of meat-eating therapsids.

Graptolites Worm-like creatures that lived in tubes.

Hadrosaurs "Duck-billed" ornithischians.

Hemichordates Wormlike relatives of the chordates.

Herbivores Animals that feed on plants.

Heterostraci A group of extinct jawless fishes.

Horned dinosaurs Rhinoceros-like ornithischians.

Ichthyosaurs Sea reptiles shaped very like dolphins.

Invertebrates Creatures without a backbone.

Jawless fishes Fishes with mouths fixed open.

Kingdom A group of related phyla (see *Phylum*).

Lepospondyls An extinct group of amphibians.

Lissamphibians The living group of amphibians.

Litopterns Extinct South American hoofed mammals.

Mammalia/Mammals Warm-blooded synapsids whose females produce milk for their young.

Mammal-like "reptiles" Extinct synapsids including the

pelycosaurs and therapsids. See *Synapsida*.

Marsupials Pouched mammals such as kangaroos.

Mesonychids A group of extinct carnivorous mammals.

Metazoans Many-celled animals with cells forming specialized tissues.

Millipedes Many-legged plant-eating arthropods.

Moas Extinct flightless birds.

Molluscs Cephalopods, bivalves, and their relatives.

Monotremes Egg-laying mammals such as the platypus.

Mosasaurs Big, extinct, sea lizards.

Neornithes Living birds and their closest ancestors.

Notochord A springy, gristly rod found in chordates.

Onychophorans Wormlike creatures with stubby legs.

Order A group of related families.

Organic compounds Chemical compounds containing carbon.

Organism A living thing.

Ornithischians The "bird-hipped" dinosaurs.

Osteichthyes Fishes with a bony skeleton rather than one made of gristle.

Osteodontorns Extinct seabirds with spiky beaks.

Paleontologist A scientist who studies prehistoric life.

Pareiasaurs A group of prehistoric anapsid reptiles.

Pelycosaurs Early mammal-like "reptiles."

Period One of the main time units in an era.

Perissodactyls The "odd-toed" hoofed mammals.

Phylum A group of related classes.

Placental mammals Mammals whose unborn young in the womb are nourished by an organ called a placenta.

Placoderms Extinct armored fishes.

Placodonts Extinct aquatic reptiles.

Plated dinosaurs Four-legged ornithischians with rows of tall plates or spines on their backs.

Plesiosaurs Big, extinct marine reptiles with flippers.

Pliosaurs Short-necked plesiosaurs.

Protorosaurs A group of early archosaurs.

Pterosaurs Skin-winged flying archosaurs.

Radiometric dating Dating certain rocks from the amounts of radioactivity that they contain.

Rauisuchians A group of carnivorous archosaurs.

Reptilia/Reptiles Tetrapods including anapsids, and diapsids such as lizards and dinosaurs.

Rhynchosaurs Plant-eating early archosaurs.

Rodents Mammals with chisel-shaped gnawing teeth.

Sarcopterygians Lobe-finned osteichthyans.

Saurischians The "lizard-hipped" dinosaurs.

Sea scorpions Extinct relatives of scorpions.

Species Any type of living thing whose individuals breed only with others of that type.

Spiny sharks See *Acanthodii*.

Stratigraphy The study of rock layers.

Synapsida/Synapsids Tetrapods with one skull hole low down below each eye. They include the extinct mammal-like "reptiles" and mammals.

Temnospondyls An extinct group of amphibians.

Terror cranes An extinct group of big flightless birds.

Tetrapods Four-legged vertebrates and their two-legged and legless descendants.

Thecodonts Various archosaurs including ancestors of the dinosaurs, pterosaurs, and crocodiles.

Therapsids Advanced mammal-like "reptiles."

Theropods The meat-eating saurischian dinosaurs.

Thorax Chest; also the middle part of an insect.

Trilobites Extinct marine arthropods like woodlice.

Uintatheres Big, extinct, horned perissodactyls.

Vertebrates Chordates with a backbone made of bones called vertebrae.

Zooid One of many tiny animals forming a colony.

Index